THE
SYNTAGMA MUSICUM
OF
MICHAEL PRAETORIUS

Da Capo Press Music Reprint Series

MUSIC EDITOR
BEA FRIEDLAND
Ph.D., City University of New York

THE
SYNTAGMA MUSICUM

OF

MICHAEL PRAETORIUS

Volume two
DE ORGANOGRAPHIA
First and Second Parts

Plus All Forty-two
Original Woodcut Illustrations from
Theatrum Instrumentorum

In an English Translation by
Harold Blumenfeld

DA CAPO PRESS • NEW YORK • 1980

Library of Congress Cataloging in Publication Data

Praetorius, Michael, 1571-1621.
    The syntagma musicum.

    (Da Capo Press music reprint series)
    Reprint of the 1962 ed. published by Bärenreiter, New York.
    1. Musical instruments.   2. Organ.
I. Title: Syntagma musicum. II. Title: De Organo-
graphia. III. Title: Theatrum instrumentorum.
ML467.P7 1979   781.9'1   79-20847
    ISBN 0-306-70563-X

This Da Capo Press edition of *Syntagma Musicum:*
Volume Two, De Organographia, First and Second Parts
is an unabridged republication of the English
translation published in New York and elsewhere
in 1962 by Bärenreiter. It is supplemented with
all forty-two original woodcut illustrations
from the *Theatrum Instrumentorum.*

Published by Da Capo Press, Inc.
A Subsidiary of Plenum Publishing Corporation
227 West 17th Street, New York, N.Y. 10011

A NOTE ON THE THIRD EDITION

This edition of Harold Blumenfeld's Englished *Syntagma Musicum* (Volume Two, *De Organographia*) contains all forty-two woodcuts — with translated captions — from Praetorius's memorable Appendix to the second volume, *Theatrum Instrumentorum*.

B. F.

THE
SYNTAGMA MUSICUM
OF
MICHAEL PRAETORIUS

Volume two
DE ORGANOGRAPHIA
First and Second Parts

In an English Translation by Harold Blumenfeld

Bärenreiter

NEW YORK / ENGLEWOOD/N.J. / CHICAGO
SAN FRANCISCO / VADUZ, LIECHTENSTEIN

PREFACE

to the English translation

Michael Praetorius was born at Kreuzberg in Thuringia in 1571. The son of a zealous Lutheran clergyman, he attended the University at Frankfort-on-the-Oder as a student of philosophy. At the age of eighteen, upon completing his studies there, he entered the service of the Duke of Braunschweig-Wolfenbüttel as chapel organist. He was made Kapellmeister at the age of thirty-three. His duties included the musical direction both of the chapel at Wolfenbüttel and of the extravagantly maintained court of the Duke, at Gröningen.

Praetorius remained at this post throughout his life. With the advance of his renown he was given many honorary duties and posts, including appointments at Halle and Dresden. The splendor and excellence of the performances and the great scope of his compositions and writings established him as the most significant German musician of the early Seventeenth Century. Hardly fifty years of age and at the height of his activity, Praetorius died at Wolfenbüttel in 1621.

It is chiefly for his writings, of which the "Syntagma Musicum" is the most significant, that Praetorius is known today. However, his musical works are exceedingly prolific. In terms of sheer quantity they represent the largest single contribution to German music of the time. Only upon his appointment as Kapellmeister did Praetorius start to compose in earnest. It is indeed remarkable that during the last few years of his life, burdened by infirmity and with the growing responsibilities attaching to his fame, he found time to set down so many works. These number in the thousands, with secular as well as sacred works of all kinds included.

Praetorius lived at a time of transition crucial for the development of German music. His period was one during which the cultural focal point in Europe was beginning to shift from the objective and worldly orientation of the Italian Renaissance towards the North, where the rising tide of mysticism and subjectivity was to arrive at its height of expression over a century later, in the High Baroque of Germany.

The changing temper of the early Seventeenth Century is manifested in music by a growing emphasis on the spectacular and colorful and in a striving towards more direct expressiveness and overt emotional effect. The changing approach to sonority which these new criteria imply find expression in the use of contrasting and opposed masses of sound and in the exploitation of spatial-acoustical effect, practises stemming from the Venetians.

In German music, the first stage in the development of the new Baroque trend completes itself in the works of Praetorius. Through his works, the new practises from the South are introduced into Germany and are absorbed into the persisting Lutheran musical tradition. Praetorius' sacred works include at once essays in the simple Lutheran chorale style, designed for the participation of an entire congregation, and works of more ambitious scope. These latter are characterized texturally by free alternation of homophonic and imitative sections. They are interspersed with instrumental ritornelli and set according to the principle of the alternation of "chori varii" — a technique in which differently constituted choirs of voices and instruments are employed alternately and simultaneously, in the interest of maximum contrast and variety of effect.

Praetorius' directions for the performance of his own works demonstrate to what a large extent the Kapellmeister was left free to adapt, arrange and orchestrate music. The written notes often served only as a general guide, with the end result left to the discretion of the conductor. The end product would often diverge widely from the original shape and textual significance of a composition.

Seen against the background of the earlier general ascendancy of the vocal and choral in music, Praetorius' instructions reflect the growth and expansion of instrumental music so significant of his times. His writings bear witness to a general fascination for sheer instrumental effect. Preoccupation with experimentation along these lines helps account for the fact that the use of voices a cappella occurs as a rather exceptional procedure during this period.

Praetorius' suggestions for the treatment of Lassus' motet, "Quo properas", written originally for ten voices in two choirs, serves to show how far the conductor of the early Seventeenth Century went towards achieving variety of color and effect:

Choir I	Choir II
1. cornet or voice, 4 trombones	cornet or voice 4 trombones
2. voices alone	cornet, 4 trombones
3. voices alone	5 viols da braccio
4. voices alone	2 flutes, 2 trombones bassoon
5. 5 viols da braccio	flute, 4 trombones
6. 5 viols da braccio	2 flutes, 2 trombones bassoon
7. 2 flutes, 2 trombones bassoon	cornet, 4 trombones

etc.

Spatial effect was also put to impressive use in the performance practise of the time. To achieve such effect — particularly in the tutti Amens and Hallelujahs — the players and singers would be disposed at different parts of the church or hall.

Praetorius sets down highly valuable indications, such as those above, in the prefaces to his musical works. It is, however, in the three-volume "Syntagma Musicum" that he subjects the new performance practises to theoretical formulation and catalogs and describes the musical instruments central to these practises.

The "Syntagma Musicum" is a work of encyclopedic scope, and was designed both as a compendium of all significant musical knowledge and as an exhaustive source on musical instruments. The first volume of the work, written in Latin and published at Wittenberg in 1615, deals chiefly with the ecclesiastical and secular music of the ancients, the instruments used in antiquity, and the music of the mass and of other Roman rites.

The second volume is in German, having been intended for a wider reading public. This volume exists in two editions printed respectively in 1618 and 1619 at Wolfenbüttel. It deals in great detail with all the musical instruments in use at the time. Particular attention is devoted to the evolution and construction of the organ. A "Theatre of Instruments" comprising forty-two woodcuts is added as an appendix to this volume. In these celebrated woodcuts, all the instruments dealt with by the author are meticulously drawn to scale.

The third volume, similarly in German, was published at Wolfenbüttel in 1619. It treats of all the secular forms of composition then practised in Italy, France, England and Germany. It deals with various theoretical matters, offers further information relative to the performance of music, and explains Italian musical terms. It establishes rules for the realization of figured basses and, finally, expostulates on the training of boys' voices after the Italian manner. Praetorius did not live to carry out a fourth volume, which was to be concerned with the theory of Zarlino, Artusi and others.

Although the "Syntagma Musicum" contains information of theoretical, historical and pedagogical interest, the emphasis throughout the work is on the practical and contemporaneous. There is little reason for designating Praetorius as a theorist, as is done in some sources, for he offers no new contributions to the body of theoretical knowledge existing in his time. When he does treat of theoretical matters, his purpose is usually a practical one and his terms are borrowed directly from theorists of his day and of earlier times.

Except for material bearing on the early development of the organ, the historically oriented passages in these volumes have little objective value. Nonetheless Praetorius' view of the musical past is colored by a quaint pedantry which makes such passages quite entertaining for the modern reader. In all justice to Praetorius let it be stated that the historical and theoretical information contained in these volumes must have been of considerable value to the readers of the author's own day.

The chief importance of the "Syntagma Musicum" today lies in the insight it affords into the character of the instruments of the time and the fashion in which they were employed. Up to the date of its appearance, this work is the most informative and exhaustive single work ever to deal with these subjects.

Most significant in this regard is the second volume, with its wood-cuts and scrupulous descriptions of the ranges, tuning and character of all instruments then employed. Because of the great interest today in the performance of earlier music, it was thought purposeful to make accessible in English these authoritative chapters on the instrumentarium of the Early Baroque. It is hoped that this translation may offer insight into the ideals of musical sound which prevailed in this era — an era which employed instruments of more subtle tone-color and of infinitely greater variety than what we are accustomed to in the present. Modern instruments, after all, represent only a handful of highly standardized versions of certain of the earlier types. The chaotically diverse instruments of the past have been taken in hand by historical forces and reduced to the several polished and perfected types so familiar to our times.

Purism in the performance of music of earlier times can be carried to false extremes. However, any musician who has had the opportunity of playing earlier music on the instruments for which it was conceived will affirm the beauty of this music and the validity of aiming to present it in its own proper terms.

The purpose served by this translation is primarily a practical one. However it was also designed to make factual and scholarly infor-mation on early instruments readily available — as Praetorius puts it, ". . . damit die Instrumenta uns zwar nich zum gebrauch, besondern zur wissenschaft auch bekant sein müchten."

Praetorius' writing is marked by a universality of approach revealing a cultured mind with a markedly academic bent. A fervent religiousness is manifested in passages which go far beyond the ordinary pious formulas proper to the written style of the time. The curiousness of Praetorius' style, reflecting a certain wilfulness and a characteristically Saxonian retractiveness of spirit, will make the reading the more entertaining in the measure that these characteristics survive in translation.

Although pleasant enough to read, Praetorius' colorful German is quite difficult to render in English. The meanings of words are inevitably obscured by the shift in connotation of their modern equivalents. Ideas are often redundantly and unclearly stated, for in this period no premium was set on economy and clarity of expression. Sentences are intricately interrelated by a maze of mutually subordinating conjunctions and littered with juxtaposed double forms of nouns and verbs — Latin terms often being used side by side with the German in order to ensure a modicum of comprehensibility.

If Praetorius found that for him it was "wegen des vielen hin- und herwiederreisens / Leibes schwachheit / und anderer grossen Beschwehrung / Unruh und viel unsäglichen verhindernüssen / unmöglich alle dinge eben so genau auf die Goldwage zu legen", it was at least attempted here. But we can join the original author in hoping that the critical reader will "alles im besten verstehen und auffnehmen", assuring that "Ist es nicht alles wohlgerahten: So ist es doch von Herzen gut und wol gemeinet".

Harold Blumenfeld
Zürich and New Haven
1949

A NOTE ON THE SECOND EDITION

The second edition of this translation has been enlarged to include ten plates from the original "Theatrum Instrumentorum". These plates were thought to hold the greatest interest for the historian and instrumentalist today. Although the number of plates included here represents only a portion of the forty-two woodcuts of the original "Theatrum Instrumentorum", it will be found that they were chosen to include representatives of most of the major groupings of instruments as outlined by Praetorius. The represented instruments include the Baroque antecedents of most contemporary instruments, and a number of the fascinating older instruments which were already obsolescent in Praetorius' day.

In the present edition, Praetorius' frequent notational illustrations have been transcribed into a readily legible form.

Harold Blumenfeld
St. Louis, August 1962

SYNTAGMA MUSICUM

of

Michael Praetorius

Second Volume

DE ORGANOGRAPHIA

therein

the Nomenclature, Tuning and Character of all Ancient and Modern
Musical Instruments, foreign, barbarian, rustic and unfamiliar as well as
indigenous, artistic, agreeable and familiar; together with true and accurate
drawings of the same.

and also

the Accurate Description of Ancient and Modern Organs, with the treatment of the manuals, pedal-board and bellows, and various manners of
tuning; also how the Regal and Harpsichord may be purely and expeditiously tuned; and what is to be paid heed to when an organ is constructed.
With a detailed register appended. And herein not only useful and necessary information for the Organist, Instrumentalist, Organ and Instrument-
maker and all Others devoted to the Muses; but also very pleasant and
agreeable reading matter for the Philosopher, Philologian and Historian.
Together with a detailed Register.

Printed in Wolfenbüttel by Elias Holwein, printer to the Prince of
Braunschweig. Published by the author.

Anno Christi MDCXIX

To Their Most Honorable, Esteemed and Learned, Most Wise and Distinguished Excellencies, the Burgomaster and Councilors of the City of

LEIPZIG

my most Gracious Masters and Mighty Patrons, etc.

Most honorable, esteemed and learned, most wise, distinguished and gracious excellencies, my mighty patrons, etc: It is much to be wondered that there is little or no information as to the kinds of wind and stringed instruments which were employed in ancient times, whether by the Hebrews for the true worship of God, or by the heathen in the execution of their superstitious rites.

Concerning the Hebrews, the material out of which their trombones were fashioned is mentioned in chap. 10 verse 2 of Numbers, where God the Almighty, in the year 2454 after Creation, commands Moses to have two trumpets made of thick silver, in order that the people might be summoned together and to give them a sign when the army was to depart. The size of these trombones was such that they could be held in one hand, as stated in chap. 7 verse 20 of Judah. However, there is no information whatever as to their form, shape and quality of sound nor about whether they could produce but one series of tones, or, as is the case with our present trombones and trumpets, many different tones. It is quite possible, however, that many tones were to be had on them, since a distinction was then made between merely sounding the trumpet, and actual trumpeting. A single trumpet was sounded when princes and generals were to be summoned before the Arc of the Covenant; and two were sounded to assemble the people there. Actual trumpeting, on the other hand, was employed at feasts for the new moon and also when camp was to be broken or battle joined in the course of war. Numbers, chap. 10 verses 3-10.

It is stated by some that the trombones used to introduce the Holy Year were made from rams' horns (Leviticus, chap. 25 verse 10) but others are of the opinion that they were of this form and shape but were actually constructed of silver or other metals.

Mention is made of pipes in Samuel, bk. I chap. 10 verse 5, and bk. II chap. 6 verse 5; in Kings, bk. I chap. 1 verse 40; in the Psalms, and in many other passages in the Scriptures. It is also described how they were employed in the anointment of kings, in bk. I chap. 1 verse 40 of Kings; for the entertainment of guests, in chap. 5 verse 15 of Isaiah; and for funeral processions, in chap. 9 verse 23 of Matthew. But no note whatever is made about the material from which they were built, their form and shape, the number of finger holes they had, nor how many tones could be produced on them.

King David did not only institute a large, well-equipped and renowned music chapel in Jerusalem, but also invented and had manufactured many instruments out of ebony. This material was brought from Ophir and had never been seen before in Palestine. These instruments must have been stringed instruments, since they were plucked. Bk. II chap. 29 verse 27 of Chronicles. Among them was the Harp—bk. I chap. 10 verses 11 and 12 of Kings—which was played by the fingers—bk. II chap. 6 verse 5 of Samuel.

That David contrived many instruments is testified in Chronicles, bk. I chap. 23 verse 5, and chap. 25 verse 7; bk. II of the same, chap. 29 verses 26 and 27; and in Josephus in bk. VII of "Antiq. Judaic." Of these instruments, several are mentioned here and there in the Psalms, but only by name, and with no information about their design and range, and the tuning of strings on eight and ten-stringed instruments.

But none the less, the music chapel of King David was four thousand strong. Of this number, 288 were directors, and these were segregated into 24 choruses, each of 12 persons, under whom were 3712 other musicians, bringing the size of each chorus to more than 150 persons. All these played on the instruments which King David had caused to be made. Bk. I of Chronicles, chap. 23 verse 5 and chap. 25 verse 7.

Solomon maintained this chapel and likewise ordered the construction of harps and psalters of ebony brought from Ophir. Bk. II of Chronicles, chap. 9 verses 10 and 11.

Hieronymus writes in a letter to Dardanus, and Josephus and Polydorus state in bk. I of Virgil's "De Inventione" that the cither of the Hebrews had 24 strings and was in the shape of a triangle, or the Greek letter Delta, the form in which some of our present instrument makers construct harps. Then there is another instrument, called by Josephus the Cynnyra, which had ten strings and was played with a plectrum; and yet another, named by him the Nablus, with twelve strings and played by the fingers. But it is not mentioned in what shape they were nor how they were tuned.

):(3

That the Hebrews did not actually describe their musical instruments is perhaps due to the fact that these were all well known to them— and it is unnecessary to write a great deal about things familiar. And furthermore, it was also because they did not wish these instruments, used in the Temple for the true worship of God the Eternal and Almighty, to be destined to the abuse of superstitious heathens in their rites—so that the pearls be not cast to the swine, as the saying goes.

About the pipes and stringed instruments of the heathens, however, the historians, poets, philologists and musicians offer somewhat more information, particularly regarding the number of holes on the pipes and strings on the stringed instruments. Certain pipes were constructed of seven separate tubes set together. Thus Virgil speaks of the "disparibus septem compacta cicutis Fistula"—the Fistula set together with seven different pipes, these producing nothing other than our seven tones, A B C D E F G—or the seven common modern musical syllables, ut re mi fa sol la si; or the bo ce di ga lo ma ni newly devised by the Belgians. Other pipes had only four holes, as M. Varro writes in bk. III of his "De Lingua Latinis", just as if he had seen them in the Temple of Marsyas with his own eyes. Still other pipes, called Spondaica, had equidistant holes; and on the pipes called Dactylica the spacing of the holes was unequal. Varro, bk. I chap. 20 of the same. The Tybia Phrygia Sinistra had two holes and the Tybia Phrygia Dextra had one, as stated by Servius in chap. 9 verse 618 of the "Aeneid" from Varro.

The Tyrrhenians had a kind of pipe comprised of two separate tubes set together. The air blown into the smaller one below entered into the larger one, stirring the water within it and thus producing a full sound. Varro, bk. I chap. 20; Julius Pollux, bk. IV.

An instrument called the Hydraulicus is described by Victruvius in bk. X. chap. 13 of his "De Architectura"; and it is said to have been invented by Ctesibius, as written in Pliny, bk. VII chap. 37, and by Ramis, in bk. I of his "Schola Mathemat.". This instrument was doubtless the forerunner of our organ.

And concerning stringed instruments, the lyre was formed in the shape of a sledge, as stated by Coelus Rhodiginus in bk. IX chap. 6 of the "Antiq. Lect.", from Ammonius Marcellinus. Its strings were at first made from linen thread, but later of gut. Bk. I chap. 48 of Varro. These strings were four in number, either after the four elements or the four seasons, or in honor of the number four itself, regarded by the Pythagoreans as a mystic quantity, and one which they used in pledging oaths, as stated by Pythagoras in the "Aureum Carmen":

> Ναì. Μὰτòν ἁμετέρα ψυχᾶ παραδ óντα
> τετραχτòν Παγὰν ἀενάσυ φύσεως

And this is to be seen at greater length in the writings of Macrobius, A. Gellius, Suida and others.

But possibly the number of these strings was in honor of the Muses, who are said to have numbered only four in the beginning; or perhaps it was after the fourfold proportions of the harmonic numbers of Pythagoras—1, 2, 3 and 4—containing in them all the ancient consonances—the unison, fourth, fifth, octave, eleventh and twelfth. Be that all as it may, the outer strings were tuned an octave apart, and the inner ones, a second apart, such that each of the latter formed a fourth with the outer string lying next it, and a fifth with the other. This is clearly represented by the harmonic numbers 6, 8, 9, 12. But this music was

):(4

very primitive up to the time of Orpheus, when the number of strings came to seven, reckoned after the number of planets or after the seven daughters of Atlantis, among them Maia, mother of Mercury, who first invented the lyre, as witnessed by Polydorus in bk. I chap. 15 of Virgil's "De Inventione".

After this, other instruments with many strings were invented— such as the forty-stringed Epigonia, after the Epigonus Ambraciota, and the Simicum, with 35 strings. These are mentioned by Julius Pollux, and by Joseph Zarlino in the introduction to Dialogue 1 of his "Demonstratione Harmoniche"; and the twenty-stringed Magadis is noted in vol. 13 of Athenaeus.

In Palestine, Asia Minor and Greece there remains no trace of any of the ancient instruments; for Mohammed, in the interest of extending his tyrannical reign, his devilish cult, and coarse inhuman barbarism, forbade throughout his land the practise of the liberal arts, conducive to friendliness, and everything else which might lead to happiness, such as wine and the playing of stringed instruments. In their place he prescribed an

f.

infernal gong, a drum, and rattling, cackling kinds of shawms. The Turks
still value these instruments highly and use them for weddings and joyful
feasts, and also in war.

When the children of the Turkish Sultan or of other great lords
are to be circumcised, the following ritual is observed:

First, two mounted Turks ride by, one with a military drum, the
other with a shawm. Then various well appointed horsemen follow, and
after them another pair of players like the first. After these is led an ox
with gilded horns slung with a rich and fragrant garland; and followed
by a large company of riders. Then more players, and again another ox
like the first, followed by many distinguished lords and knights. Next a
group of glistening janissaries on foot, among them the Sultan's son, to be
circumcised. And finally, many musicians with drums and shawms
follow to the church.

And when a Christian is converted to a Mameluk or Turk and
submits himself to circumcision, he is set on a beautiful horse and led
through the whole city with a shawming and drumming. Still today this
shabby music is held in great esteem by the Turks, while ours is despised
in the extreme. Once King Francis I of France honored the Turkish
bloodhound Solymanno, whose reign started in 1520 A. D. (but in the
year 926 of the Moslem era) by presenting him with a large and fine
organ, which, to the wonderment of the Turks, was difficult even for
several men to carry; and with this he also sent several choice and skilled
musicians. The Turkish sultan was at first well pleased, but soon thereafter
in Constantinople, when the people came in swarms to hear these fine
foreign musicians and won very great devotion to their art, the sultan
became concerned lest through this music his people might lose their coarse
barbarian ways and become soft and effeminate. Thus he had this fine
instrument broken to pieces and cast to the flames, sending the musicians
back home again to the Frenchman.

But a detailed report of all this is to be found in the first volume
of this "Syntagma Musicum", and I regard it unnecessary to treat it in
greater detail here.

Although there is little or no information about the form and design, holes or strings, and tuning of ancient instruments, in this Second Volume I have humbly endeavored to publish drawings of the fine and artful instruments presently used in Germany, Italy, France and England, with information about their tuning and range as well.

Instrumentalists may then learn from this how wind and stringed instruments are to be used in sets and tuned; and conductors may also observe what types of instruments are suitable in range for the rendering of the various voices in ensemble music.

Then I have also wanted to include drawings of foreign, rustic and primitive instruments, some used in Muscovy, Turkey and Arabia, others in India and America, in order that we Germans might have some information about them, even though no knowledge of how they are played.

And similarly as not much is to be found about organs in historical writings, I have also wished to indicate here, in so far as I am able, how the present modern organ developed from time to time out of the early organ, both in respect to pipes and their various registers, and the bellows, wind-chambers, manual and pedalboards, etc. In a corollary I have shown how the Regal and Harpsichord may be purely and expeditiously tuned and what is to be paid heed to when an organ is constructed; and I have also included information about the distribution of many famed organs.

For because your most worthy excellencies are particularly great fosterers of music and regard it with esteem and devotion—in that distinguished men have always served Music in your most praiseworthy Schools, among them George Rhaw, who once composed a mass for twelve voices and performed it before a great assembly in the Thomaskirche, receiving great praise for it, and who later, in the year 1530, circulated his "Musica Practica" in two volumes, a work which is also consulted by the Italians. Then further there was Johannes Gallicus, who was so well versed in musical practise that in the year 1520 he had his treatise, "De Compositione Cantus", published. And in the interest of brevity not naming others, I wish to observe with all due respect and honor, the memory of the skilled and superb mathematician, musician and chronologist, the late Seth Calvisius, whose work has gained him an immortal name and who was also the teacher of the excellent M. Johannes Lippius—who would have been able to publish many additional writings for the benefit of our common Fatherland, had he not been summoned prematurely from this life; but whose position has now been filled by another distinguished practical musician and composer, Johann Hermann Schein. I am of the opinion that the gifted mathematician and music theorist, Henricus Baryphonus from Verniggerode in Lower Saxony (1), Music Director and Cantor at Quedlinburg, will notably follow the example of the mentioned excellent Calvisius, particularly in what concerns music theory; and that he will shortly publish his music-theoretical works, to the great service of the German Nation. Many distinguished persons are already waiting for these works with anticipation.

And while my humble and undeserving person has enjoyed the high grace, favorable disposition and beneficence of your most worthy excellencies, for which I could find no suitable opportunity up to now to express my gratitude, it therefore occurred to me to present this quite insignificant work to your excellencies, thus placing myself before you as one who would be grateful. And although this work itself is neither large nor notable, I pray that your graces will not regard the work alone, but also consider the grateful heart and good intentions of its author, accepting the will before the deed; and further that your graces will be and remain the masters, patrons and promoters of myself and of mine. I set this trust firmly in your excellencies, to whom I am ever ready to dedicate my willing services according to my modest abilities; and whom I hereby salutarily and faithfully commend to the heavenly protection of God.

Dated the 19th of June, on which date 1294 years ago the Council of Nicea commenced, which, convoked by Constantine the Great, protected three hundred and eighteen bishops from the vile heresy of Arianus, and which also decreed that "sicut erat in principio, et nunc et semper, et in secula seculorum, Amen" be added to the versicle "Gloria Patri et Filio et Spiritui Sancto" in church. In the year 1619 after the Birth of

Christ, in the common reckoning, and 1621 after the true calculation; 5568 years after the Creation of the World, 3912 after the Deluge, 3116 after the Exile from Egypt; and 2371 after the Founding of the City of Rome; and in the 599th Olympiad.

Your Honorable, Most Worthy and Magnificent Excellencies'

most humble servant,

Michael Praetorius of Kreuzberg

To all Organists, Instrumentalists, Organ and Instrument
Makers and all Those who Play and are Fond of Instrumental Music, of Germany and Other Nations as well:

the author extends his greetings and wishes all good fortune, blessings
and welfare; and prays obligingly that each will accept and note with
good will this his well-intentioned labor, compiled with not a little effort
and expense from authoritative writings and out of his own diligent
research and experience; and trusts that he will not be regarded as wishing
to vulgarize the Art of Music by publishing this work in our German
mother tongue and thus exposing it to every ignorant blockhead and
bungler. The author has already been reproached by certain shallowly
learned wiseacres, and unduly, to be sure; for this work was not intended
to be a sort of Vestal Mystery to be kept from the unhallowed multitude
(as the poet says); nor was it to be used as a philosophers' touchstone and
regarded as an occult mystery. Nor does it set forth the reason for the
fact that the sound of pipes caused the Isles of the Nymphs in Lydia to
separate from the mainland and move to the middle of the sea, making
crosswise movements there as if dancing, and then returning to their place
on the shore—all of which M. Varro declares as if he had witnessed it
with his own eyes.

The author is well aware that the first volume of this work was
published in Latin, and the second and third volumes might fittingly have
followed similarly. But he decided to print these latter in German, because in modern languages, particularly Italian and German, many terms
are employed which cannot be brought into clear Latin terminology. The
translation of such terms would render the language obscure and difficult
to comprehend, and this would not be of any great benefit to organ and
instrument makers, who generally are not well versed in this language.

):(5

Thus in this book and all his other works, the author has intended
to put to the service of our common German Fatherland the gifts and
talent bestowed on him by God, Lord of Mercy, and has wished herewith

to leave behind a memorial to Posterity—close as this transitory world may be approaching its end—in setting down the various kinds of musical instruments which are presently employed in the church and in imperial, royal, electoral and princely chapels, and used to the Glory of God and for the blissful cheering of our human hearts in this our last remaining time.

It would also be desirable to know what actual kinds of musical instruments and ecclesiastical organs were found in the times of David and Solomon and before and after them as well, and how each instrument was really constructed and tuned; but unfortunately no such information has come down to us in old sources, and thus ancient instrumental music remains little known to us, or completely unknown.

In certain libraries a book may be found which was printed in quarto at Basel in 1511 and which contains drawings of several ancient and modern instruments. But this work is not actually very old, and nothing particular is to be gleaned from it about the use and character of the diagramed instruments.

On this account the author hopes that ignorants such as those mentioned above, will change their minds for the better when they take note of how many works of science and art have been published in the service of posterity by distinguished doctors, surgeons, mathematicians, geometricians, painters, and others exercised in the liberal arts; and that they will be more favorably inclined towards the author's well-intentioned labor, designed for the general profit of all. It can also very well happen that hereafter other and more excellent people, with a thorough knowledge of the writings of musicians, historians and philosophers, may thus find cause markedly to improve this poor account and meager guide and to present it in a clearer and more complete form. To beginners, however, the author hopes herewith to have given some incitement to further research and reflection; and in so far as he may have erred in one thing or another in these present works and in his earlier works as well, or should he have recorded too much or too little, still he does not doubt that reasonable souls will be found who will accept and interpret everything in the best light and whose judgement will not be influenced by any feelings of envy, misfavor or antipathy which they might without cause bear him; and he hopes that they will also take into account that due to much travelling about, to frailty of body, great hardship, anxiety, and other unutterable hindrances, it may not have been possible for him to weigh each of his words quite justly. And persons who think of nothing but how to find fault with an honest man, and who regard only their own accomplishments as worthy and reputable, ought justly to take all this into consideration, lest they be reproached with the old proverb, "Hic Rhodus, hic salta". And then, be this as it may, the author is reminded of the maxim, "Ne Jovem quidem, sive serenum sive pluvium, omnibus placere posse". The author wishes herewith to commend himself to the benevolence and favor of all honest and upright musicians and lovers of music, organists and organ makers, offering all his willing services so long as God the Beloved affords him life.

Fear of the Lord is the Commencement of Wisdom (2)

MDCXIX

):(6

this
ORGANOGRAPHIA
or Second Volume

is comprised of Five Parts.

In the First Part
is treated
the Nomenclature of Musical Instruments.

The classification of all musical instruments in present use and their consideration according to kind—pp. 1-8, with appended table—p. 10.

In the Second Part,
the Range and Properties of Musical Instruments.

The various ranges of all wind and stringed instruments; their pitch; the extreme high and low notes to be obtained from them according to their size and character; and in an appended table, explanation of the peculiarities of each instrument.

1.   How the terms, Instrument, Instrumentalist (3); Accord, Sorts; and Falsetto Tones, as on pipes and other instruments, are to be understood. pp. 11-13.

2.   Of the pitch proper to the organ and other instruments, and to the human voice; and of the difference between choral pitch and chamber pitch. pp. 14-17.

3. & 4. A Universal Table, therein the clef and note signs, the range of tones in scale, and the measure of tones in feet (in the fashion of organ makers) for all instruments. pp. 18-30.

Wind Instruments

| 5. | Tromboni | Posaunen | Trombones | pp. 31, 32 |

o.

46. Various Ancient Instruments

In the Third Part
the History of Early Organs

About the first invention of the early organ, the arrangement of its keyboards, sounding-board, bellows, etc. Also how it was improved in all
this from time to time until it reached its present state.

):(7

1. Of the dignity and excellence of the organ.

Let it be mentioned here that it would be very desirable if organists devoted to their noble art with profound earnestness, zeal and
diligence, were to be provided with better wages and maintenance, rather
than being regarded as lower and more contemptible than the meanest
artisans. For in David's time comparable church musicians were made
Levites and priests, and in ecclesiastical rank they stood second only to
the actual clergy. If King David, before all others a great patron of
musicians and himself a superior music director, had been able to hear the
excellent organists now working in certain communities, doubtless he would
not have known how to extoll and elevate them high enough. At the
present time certain organists, and good ones to be sure, must somehow
manage with a yearly salary of 50, 40 or 30 thaler, and even less; and
I can but wonder how such good people are able to maintain themselves
and often wives and children as well. People listen with great pleasure
when an able and skilled organist beautifully and pleasingly treats sacred
Latin and German songs and psalms, making the heart jubilate with inner

joy, fervor and attentiveness, and rousing it for the sermon following. Therefore each authority, city councilor and father of the Church, and the members of every community as well, should all take justly into account that such servants of the Church ought to be held in greater esteem and provided with better subsistence, salary and maintenance.

I humbly pray that these remarks will not be regarded unfavorably.

2. How long organs have been in use and who first invented them.

3. Of the smaller early organs, and the voices, etc, which they had.

4. Of the ensuing medium sized organs.

5. How and when the pedal was invented.

6. Of the large old organs.

7. Of the arrangement of the keyboards on old organs, and the kind of sound produced on them.

8. Of the pitch of old organs, and how the keys of the pipes were arranged.

9. Of the bellows of those times.

10. Of the various names for old organs.

11. Of the difference between earlier and modern organs.

12. In what form and how the sliding chest was made.

13. The keyboards.

14. How the voices and pipes were altered and increased in number until brought to a better state in the present time.

in the Fourth Part
the History of Modern Organs.

I.   Of the correct names for our present modern organs, according to their proportions and the size of their diapasons.

II.   Of the various kinds of voicings on the organ and their terminology; and how the same are correctly to be understood according to their sound and character. Also how in general such voices may variously be calculated from the length of their body and according to the number of feet of their various low and high-pitched tones. With further and more exhaustive report on what in particular must be known regarding each kind of voicing — such as the measure or length of the pipes and the distribution of the pipes. With appended universal table.

Then the following will be treated:
1.   Open stops like diapasons.
2.   Holflutes and their character.
3.   Gemshorn, blockflute, spitzflute and flat-flute stops.
4.   Quintatone, nacht-horn and cross-flute stops.
5.   Covered stops of all kinds.
6.   Rohrflutes.
7.   Open reed stops.
8.   Closed reed stops.
):(8

III.   Instructions as to how organ reed stops and regals are to be tuned; also how instruments such as the harpsichord spinet and others of their like may be properly and purely tuned, and how the other pipes of the organ are adjusted.

IV.   That those who wish to have an organ built in their church to the honor of our Lord God, should take care to look about for experienced and reputable organ makers and not be misled by the paltry advantage in price which they might gain from novice and inexperienced organ makers. Yet, even if an organ maker is experienced, still there is no assurance that the organs he attends to will not be unreliable and in need of constant repair.

1.   The arrangement and listing of all stops and registers of the most famous organs in Germany.

2.   A detailed index and register.

3.   How a pitch-pipe can be made from wood or metal and tuned to the correct choral pitch, so that it can be used when necessary.

in the Sixth Part
a Sciagraphia or Theatre of Instruments.

True likenesses and drawings, cut in wood, of each and every musical instrument both ancient and modern, foreign and native, with the size, length and breadth of the same accurately drawn to scale; with the drawings distributed among some forty woodcuts.

With appended index and register.

Of the Harmonious Unity of Sacred Music

Here and in the Third Volume, mention is made of the highly important fact that cantors and organists occupying public church office ought closely to cooperate in arranging the succession of pieces for the service, so that they can work together in fitting consent and unity of purpose, each always executing his part of the music in the proper choral pitch and bringing it to its end in the correct key. This in order that the music not become confused and cause annoyance to God and His Christian Laity, and lest the cantor and organist might prejudice themselves thereby. For when the organist does not play in the proper key, and particularly when he transposes a piece by a second or third, in disregard of the cantor, everything must either go too high with a squeaking and a squealing, or too low, with a rumbling and grumbling. This alters the way in which the modes move the affections and creates chaos among the singers and players of the ensemble. And when such a thing comes to pass, if the cantor is well trained he surely will not take the pitch from the organist, but will find it from a pitch-pipe or with his own ear, and will intone the pitch of the correct key once the organ has finished. This is vexatious to hear in church, and what is worse, it also confounds the boy singers: for while the key in which the organ has played remains fresh in the consciousness of the boys, they are seldom able to make the change in key without confusion and cannot find the newly intoned key until the previous key of the organ has left their mind. Not to mention that such an occurrence is also very annoying for the accompanying instrumentalists; for when the cantor takes the wrong key from the organist and begins the chorus in it before the players enter and before they can blow into their cornets or trombones and establish the correct pitch, the instruments — especially cornets and violins — cannot come in when they are supposed to, for the players are not familiar with transposition by the second and third. To be sure, it is difficult and onerous enough for some of them just to transpose a part by a fourth or fifth, and even this simple transposition often engenders confusion and results in pitiful playing.

And with unpleasant, ill-sounding, dissonant music such as this, the organist and cantor profane the Holy Ear and Countenance of God, insult the Christian congregation, desecrate public worship not a little, heavily offend God the Lord as a God of Order, and do themselves harm besides; and not without vexing many devout Christian hearts and also

):(9

provoking the scornful contempt and contemptuous scorn of others. And due to the inordinate wisdom and cleverness, insatiable pride, jealousy and vengeful obstinacy—inspired by the Archfiend—of the one toward the other, the like of this unfortunately is wont to occur in some—though, God be praised, few—of our communities. Of course, obdurate organists and cantors of this kind inflict the greatest part of the damage on themselves in thus exposing themselves to the disfavor of their superiors and of all God-loving people; and when they do not refrain from their tiresome competitiveness and from such ugly behavior in church—even after having been admonished, it eventually costs them their position. Reasonable and discreet organists, however, are not at all intended here.

Harmoniae vocum addictos, Harmonicis
Consonare decet cordibus ac animis.
Concordia enim res parvae crescunt:
Discordia maximae dilabuntur.

II.   It occurs to me that several churches and communities have
requested copies of my Latin works published four years ago, including the
Missodia, Hymnodia, Megalodia, and Eulogia (most of which may well be
used as motets). But because of lack of funds for the necessary materials,
it was not possible to reprint them. So now, to the Honor of God and
for the Extolling of His Name—towards which alone all my works and
labors have been directed—I wish to declare myself ready and most
willing to supply copies of the mentioned works, of my present large Opus
Polyhymnis III Panegyricae, and what copies still may remain of my
German Musae Sioniis, Uranodia and Litania, to any of those who
request them on order of the clergymen of their community, in so far as
no expense is occasioned therewith to me and mine. However, lest anyone
should irresponsibly attempt to obtain any of this music for the sake of
trade and gain, I shall place legal responsibility on each recipient of the
music delivered. (For the like of this has occurred in the past, and I myself
have come across cases in which certain individuals who had received
music from me sold it for money or traded it at other places without
delivering it. To be sure, I should have liked to send the last parts of the
Musae Sioniis and other things to various localities, but the messengers
acted so disgracefully that I had to give up the matter.)

Included in the mentioned Latin and German works are the following listed works:

In the Missodia:

1.   10 Kyries and 5 In Terra Pax.

2.   Diverse Dominus Vobiscum, etc; Praefationes, Sanctus, Agnus Dei,
Amens and Glorias.

3.   a Missa Sine Nomine and a Discubuit Jesus for 8 voices.

In the Hymnodia:

24 Hymns with almost all the verses set differently, for use throughout the entire year; each hymn conveniently to be used as a motet.

In the Megalodia:

14 Magnificats for 5, 6 and 8 voices.

):(10

In the Eulogodia:

17 various Bene-Deodicamus, In Natale Domini, Resonet in Laudibus, Completoria, Regina Coeli, Salve Regina for 2, 3, 4, 5, 6 and 8 voices; all in the manner of the motet, such that they may be performed in place of motets.

In the Urania:

various German sacred songs for 2, 3 or 4 choirs and quite plainly set in simple counterpoint, note against note, such that the congregation can join in the singing. More in regard to this may be found in the preface to the work.

In the Litania:

1. the Lesser Litany, Nimm von uns Herr Gott.
2. the Greater Litany, Kyrie, Christe Eleison, etc.
3. a setting of Erhalt Uns Herr bei Deinem Wort, all arranged for 5, 7 and 8 voices in two choirs.

Regarding the German psalms and sacred songs contained in the Polyhymnia III Panegyrica, and the various novel kinds of settings in the Italian manner, also at hand in this volume, information may be found in the article on Figured Bass and elsewhere in Book Three of "Syntagma Musicum", pp. 175, 176 et fol, and 202, 203, etc.

The Polyhymnia Exercitatrix (see p. 207 of bk. three) has been published in Frankfort on the Main this year. It contains various Halle-lujahs and other songs written for the purpose of giving chorus boys exercise in singing and for accustoming them to the present Italian manner. These pieces may also be played as canzoni by 5 or 6 stringed or wind instruments without the use of voices. Until now, these pieces have never appeared in print.

The Polyhymnia IV Puericinia (see p. 205 of bk. three) contains 14 concert pieces in a quite unfamiliar style, in which three or four boys sing together at first, with the other voices and the instruments entering later in the tutti. And the Praeambulum Jubilaeum (see pp. 210, 211 of bk. three) contains 11 concert pieces written in still another unique and new fashion, with sinfonias and other instrumental pieces.

And then also various secular pieces.

All this will come forth in print this year in Frankfort and Leipzig, God willing.

Should some cantors and musicians misinterpret or perhaps misjudge my treatment of various subjects at first, and be prone to cavil and raise objections to one thing or another, I pray that they will contact me by letter or in person about any faults they may find and learn my reply. But should I in the meanwhile be summoned from this earth in accordance with the will of God, I doubt not that there will be good people at Dresden, Halle, Leipzig, Quedlinburg and elsewhere to whom the new manner is well known and who will both defend my standpoint and express it more clearly and expansively.

):(11

I have only intended this work as a modest guide and meant just to lay the ground-work with it. On this, more excellent musicians may continue to build to the best of their ability, bringing the structure to completion and keeping it up to date. For perhaps due to weakness and other causes, I may not be able entirely to complete certain articles promised in my writings—among them those dealing with Figured Bass and the Construction of Organs. In view of this, I sincerely hope that the esteemed musician and lover of sacred music will be kindly disposed towards me as one who at first was occupied with the liberal arts and who only quite late arrived at the practise of music; and towards my musical works, written by the Grace of God within a period of sixteen years and partly printed at my own expense, partly withheld for revision. And since because of infirmity, continual travelling and many other difficulties, it was not possible to set down everything quite elaborately and perfect in every detail, I pray I will be forgiven out of Christian charity; and if I have not succeeded in all, still my intentions were earnest.

And may the gracious Lord look compassionately down on us as our coarse voices and wagging tongues intone the canticles of praise and prayer of the holy patriarchs, prophets and apostles in this our transitory life; and in the eternal divine life now approaching, when we rejoice and sing together with all the divine singers and angels and archangels before the throne of the Lord, may He help us to hold with them an everlasting concert, celebrating with alternating choruses the joyous marriage of Our Holy Groom, Jesus Christ, extolling God the Lord and the indivisible Trinity with our joyous shout of praise, singing with the Cherubim and Seraphim the most exquisite and beautiful words of the Sanctus, "Holy, holy, holy is God the Lord of Hosts"; and joyfully joining in without the least confusion and flaw when the angels intone a song of the Nativity of Christ the Lord, singing "Gloria in Excelsis Deo"—Glory to God in the Highest; and singing and playing the Canticum Agni—the Song of the Lamb—with the Elders of the Revelation of Saint John, with harps and cymbals: "Te decet laus, te decet hymnus, tibi debetur omnis honor, tibi virtus et fortitudo, Domino Deo nostro in secula": and thus praise and glorify the Kingdom and the Power and the Salvation and the Might of Christ our God for ever and ever. Amen, Amen.

Ad Clarassimum & Celeberrimum avi nostri Musicum

Michaelem Praetorium,

Capellae Electoralis Saxonicae Dresdensis, Archiepiscopalis
Magdaeburgensis & Guelpherbytanae Brunovicensis,
Directorem & Choragum Solertissimum.
Anagrammatismus.

Michael Praetorius
Hic Iam Alter Orpheus.

Hic Iam, Musarum decus, Alter, dicitur, Orpheus,
Pieridum docta qui regit arte Chorum.
Luxuriante leves qui tangit pollice chordas,
Et cujus dulcitempla canore sonant.
Omne tulit punctum: docet hoc, quod doctus Apollo
Indelibata condidit ante via.
Qui sic? Nam vigili prospexit ad omnia sensu,
Hinc est multorum maxima cura Ducum   ):(12
Hinc secum ducit summa cum laude Camaenas,
Quae tristes mulcent voce sonante viros.
Hinc animo crescit virtus, hinc splendor honore
Culmen Praetori laudis utrumque tenes.
Testor! sed non es proprii jactator honoris,
Fastidis strepitus: Te tua Musa vehit.
Artem rimatus multo sudore latentem,
Quam tibi dat tersae nobile mentis opus.
Hos raros libros oculorum indagine lustra,
Rebus in adversis dulce levamen erunt.
Buccina, Bombyces, Tuba, Tibia, Bassanelli,
Organa, Systra, lyrae, Barbitos atque Chelys.
Sambucae, Crotalum, Pandura, Theorba, Penorcon,
Cymbala, Nabla, fides, Tympana, Crembla, Chorus.
Omnia Phoebeae si quae sunt plectra Cohortis,
Sint tibi laetitiae, causa, caputque tuae.
Hic labor, hoc opus est vel Phoebo judice dignum
Transvolet Eoas, occiduasque plagas.
Felices animi qui sic clarescere tentant,
Non horum virtus indiga laudis erit.

Μουσικοφιλίας ergo
admodulabatur Collegium Musicum Quedlinburgense

1618   OranDVM   ⎫
1619   PoenItenDVM ⎬ ChrIstVs appropInqVabIt
1620   o VenI DoMIne IesV Christe VenI
1623   ah koM HErr IesV Christe / DV eVVIger Sohn Gottes.

First Part

of this

SECOND VOLUME

The General Description of Musical Instruments in use at the present time; their Names, Classification and Differences.

I

Musical instruments may be described as the ingenious work of able and earnest artisans who devised them after much diligent thought and work, fashioned them out of good materials and designed them in the true proportions of art, such that they produce a beautiful accord of sound and can be employed for the magnification of God and the fitting and proper entertainment of men.

II

Musical instruments can only be classified and differentiated in terms of their pitch and sound—firstly, quo ad qualitativem generationem, by examining how and with what kind of motion of the instrument and of the human limbs their sound is generated, and secondly—quo ad quantitativem generationem, by measuring their range in pitch.

III

Now regarding the generation of sound in musical instruments, certain instruments are made to sound when air is introduced into their chambers. These are named Instrumenta ἔμπνευσα or wind instruments.

IV

But a distinction is made among them, for some are made to sound by the air of Nature; others by the human breath.

V

Of the first kind are those instruments in which air is introduced into pipes by means of bellows, namely:

> organum portabile or portative organ—an organ which can be played while being carried.
>
> positivum or positive
>
> regale or regal

These could be called piped instruments.

VI

Those blown with the human breath are called Inflatilia, or blown wind instruments. Of these, certain are sounded without any moving of the instrument, namely:

> tuba or trumpet.

Certain others, however, are operated by the hand or regulated by the fingers as well, and are either without holes, such as the

> buccina or trombone,

the slides of which must be drawn in and out by the hand; or have holes which are covered and uncovered by the fingers as required by the tones of a melody.

VII

The latter, instruments with holes, are again of three kinds. The first have holes on the front of their tubes; the second, on front and back; the third, on front, back and on the sides.

VIII

Of the first kind, which only have holes in front and none in back, there are again two varieties: those with wind bags, such as the

      tibia utricularis or bagpipe,

and those without wind bags, such as the

      fiffari, tibia transversa or traversa: cross flute or fife.

      lituus or shawm

      piffari or small alto bumbarde

IX

Of the second kind, namely with holes on front and back, are these:

      corno, cornetto: a curved black cornet

      cornamuti or straight yellow cornet

      cornamuse or krummhorn

      tibia, fistula, flauti: flutes or recorders

      fagotti, dolciane: bassoons and dulcians

      bombyces: a large bass bumbarde and other bumbardes

      bassanelli and certain bagpipes such as the Bock, Hümmelchen, Dudey, etc.

X

To the third kind, with holes on front and back and on the sides as well, belong these:

      racketts, sordunes, doppioni and schryari.

XI

And the above are, then, ἔμπνευσα, inflata, or piped wind instruments. Now follow the instruments named ἄπνευσα or specifically, κρούσα, percussa, or percussion instruments. These are instruments which are struck by means of wooden sticks and other objects. Among them, distinction is made between those without strings, ἄκορδα and those with strings, ἔγκορδα.

XII

Those without strings are made to sound by striking only, and this is accomplished:

1. by iron or wooden sticks or beaters, as on the:

   tympanum or kettledrum

   crepitaculum or triangle

   clavitympanum or strawfiddle (6)

2. or by bell clappers or tiny metal globes, as on:

   campanae or bells

   tintinnabula or small bells

   cymbala or cymbals

   sistra

   nolae or sleighbells

XIII

Of the instruments called ἔγκορδα, fidicinia, or stringed instruments, some have gut strings made from the intestines of animals, particularly of sheep, and others have metal strings made of steel, silver, iron, brass or other material.

XIV

Of the instruments with gut strings,

1. certain are played and controlled by the fingers alone, such as the:

   testudo, chelys or lute

   theorbo, like a large bass lute. (Description of this instrument is to be found in the second part of this second volume of "Syntagma Musicum")

   quinterna or quintern

   arpa, psalterium or harp.

2. certain are stroked by a haired bow at the same time, such as the:

lyra, lyrone: or Italian lyra

arce-violate lyra: or large lyra

viole da gamba: or viols da gamba

violino, rebecchino, fides, fidicula: or small violin, also
called viol da braccio

viola bastarda

chorus or tympanischiza: trummscheit or trumpet marine.
(This latter is an instrument of considerable length, much like a wooden
board, and has four strings which are stroked by a bow, producing a
sound as of four trumpets and a clarino all together. More about this in
the Second Part.)

    3. There is also an instrument played by keys and with a wheel
to set its strings into motion in place of a bow, namely the

lyra rustica or pagana: the common lyra (7)

XV

The instruments just enumerated have gut strings, as was stated. Now
follow those with metal strings. These are made to sound by being
struck in the following ways:

    1. just with the fingers alone, as on the

pandora, penorcon, orpheoreon and harpa irlandica or
Irish harp;

    2. by means of a feather quill, as on the
cithara or cither

    3. by means of raven feathers fit into wooden jacks, as on the
various Instrumenta—that is specifically, the

virginals, spinet, harpsichord and clavicytherium, all generally referred to as Instruments (3); and the arpi-
chordium and clavichord.

    4. by means of a wooden stick, as on the
sambuca, barbytus: or dulcimer

XVI

All the instruments recounted up to here might be called primary
instruments, in distinction to the next, which have actually developed
from the foregoing. Of these are the following:

    1. the Claviorganum, an instrument on which not only pipes are

made to sound by means of bellows, but also strings are struck by feather quills, all producing a very lovely sound.

    2. the Crembalum, a Jews harp, which, when it is to be played, requires human breath as in the second kind of wind instruments, and is struck by the finger at the same time. These instruments might be called mixed instruments.

XVII

And so much for the consideration of the sound of musical instruments according to the manner in which it is generated and the way it is made on the instruments. Now we must further examine their sound in terms of their measurement, and this in the following ways:

    1. respectu longitudinis—how long the tone can be held and whether it is fixed in tuning.

    2. respectu latitudinis—which instruments can be made to produce all tones and execute all voices of a piece; which instruments afford only certain voices; and which yield only a single voice at a time.

    3. respectu profunditatis vel elevationis et depressionis—which instruments can be brought outside their natural range and which cannot.

XVIII

Firstly, regarding musical instruments in respectu longitudinis, we find that

    1. certain instruments are tuned to fixed pitches which vary little even though the instruments be put to continual use. These include all the percussion instruments named, and also certain piped instruments, such as the organ and positive.

    2. on other instruments the tuning may easily and frequently be modified and changed. Of the wind instruments blown by the mouth, this includes the tibia utricularis or bagpipe. And almost all stringed instruments are included here, among them the cithara, pandura, penorcon, orpheoreon, and arpa hybernica, all with metal strings; and the arpa communis or common harp, testudo or lute, theorbo, viols, violins, lyras, etc. with gut strings. The instruments with gut strings go out of tune more easily than those with metal strings because gut expands or contracts, depending on the weather, more readily than steel and brass.

3. some instruments, however, stand between the first two kinds, their tuning being neither as constant as that of the first nor as variable as that of the second. Here are included the tympanum or drum, regal, clavichord, harpsichord and spinet.

XIX

Secondly, regarding the sound of instruments in respectu latitudinis or with respect to the number of tones which they can be made to produce at a time, we find

1. instrumenta παντόνα, omnivoca or omnisona; or fully voiced instruments on which all parts of a piece can be played, and which I call fundament instruments because they must be used as a fundament when a single part is sung or played together with them. These include the organ, regal, harpsichord, virginals, lute, harp, double cither, pandora, penorcon and the like.

2. instrumenta πολύτονα, multivoca or multisona, on which several parts may be played, but not all — such as the cithara parva and lyra parva da braccio and lyra da gamba.

3. instrumenta μονότονα, univoca or unisona; or single—voiced instruments which can only contribute a single part in ensembles. Included here are all instruments blown by the mouth, such as the trombone, cornet, flute, shawm and the like; and also certain stringed instruments, such as the violin and the like. In the Third Volume these are named Ornament Instrumenta.

XX

Thirdly and last, regarding the sound of instruments in respectu profunditatis, or with respect to range, we find:

1. instruments which do not readily yield tones outside their natural range. Here are included all stringed and percussion instruments and various wind instruments, particularly those with pipes.

2. instruments on which experienced players, with the help of lips and embouchure, are able to produce tones somewhat above or below their natural range. The peculiarities of each of these instruments in this respect will be treated later in greater detail.

A special table of all instruments should here be at hand, but since it might be rather awkward in German, reference is made instead to the four various synopses and tables to be found at the end of part two of the First Volume.

And though one must make distinctions between instruments in many different respects, we wish to classify them here in two principal ways, namely:

as Inflatilia or Tibicinia; and as Fidicinia—
that is, as Wind and Stringed Instruments, and in Italian, as
instrumenta da fiato and da chorde.

And these will all be treated
now in the Second Part.

Second Part

of this

SECOND VOLUME

Of Wind and Stringed Instruments of various kinds, and their Range in accordance with their size and character.

therein

1.   What is to be understood by the terms Instrument and Instrumentist (3); Accord and Sorts; and Falsetto Tones, as of flutes and other instruments (9).

2.   Of the pitch proper to the organ and other instruments, and to the human voice; and of the difference between choral pitch and chamber pitch.

3.   A Universal Table, therein the Claves Signatae or clef-signs, the Claves in Scala Tabulaturae, or notation of the tones of the gamut, applying to all instruments; and the foot number of the tones reckoned in the fashion of the organ maker.

4.   Report on everything treated in this table.

N B   I believe it advisable to insert here a table in which all instruments treated in the following forty-four chapters are listed according to kind.

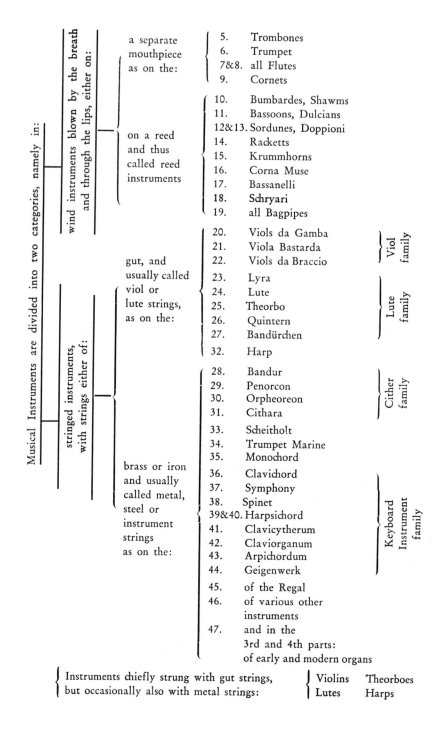

Musical Instruments are divided into two categories, namely in:

wind instruments blown by the breath and through the lips, either on:

a separate mouthpiece as on the:

5.	Trombones
6.	Trumpet
7&8.	all Flutes
9.	Cornets

on a reed and thus called reed instruments

10.	Bumbardes, Shawms
11.	Bassoons, Dulcians
12&13.	Sordunes, Doppioni
14.	Racketts
15.	Krummhorns
16.	Corna Muse
17.	Bassanelli
18.	Schryari
19.	all Bagpipes

stringed instruments, with strings either of:

gut, and usually called viol or lute strings, as on the:

20.	Viols da Gamba	} Viol family
21.	Viola Bastarda	
22.	Viols da Braccio	
23.	Lyra	} Lute family
24.	Lute	
25.	Theorbo	
26.	Quintern	
27.	Bandürchen	
32.	Harp	

brass or iron and usually called metal, steel or instrument strings as on the:

28.	Bandur	} Cither family
29.	Penorcon	
30.	Orpheoreon	
31.	Cithara	
33.	Scheitholt	
34.	Trumpet Marine	
35.	Monochord	
36.	Clavichord	} Keyboard Instrument family
37.	Symphony	
38.	Spinet	
39&40.	Harpsichord	
41.	Clavicytherum	
42.	Claviorganum	
43.	Arpichordum	
44.	Geigenwerk	
45.	of the Regal	
46.	of various other instruments	
47.	and in the 3rd and 4th parts: of early and modern organs	

Instruments chiefly strung with gut strings, but occasionally also with metal strings:

Violins   Theorboes

Lutes   Harps

I

What is to be understood by the terms, Instrument and Instrumentalist; Accord and Sorts; and Falsetto Tones, as of flutes and other instruments (9).

In order to avoid all error which might originate in the varying use of the terms Instrumentalist and Instrument, the following must be made clear. Although the word Instrument is commonly used to designate key-board instruments such as the harpsichord, spinet, virginals and the like, this is inaccurate and ought not to occur. Similarly the use of the word Instrumentalist is false when it is made to apply only to one who plays on such instruments.

The word Instrument refers quite generally to all musical instruments alike, particularly single-voiced instruments like cornets, trombones, flutes and violins, etc. This term is not to be restricted just to a few fully-voiced instruments. And thus it follows that players of the harpsichord ought to be referred to as organists and not as instrumentalists.

And even though the organ is called an instrument of instruments, on account of its excellence, and while it contains the voices of almost all other instruments (see first part of the article on early organs) it still is not acceptable to designate it by the word, instrument. This would occasion great confusion and inconsistency, for at all court chapels it is the practise to designate as instrumentalists all those who execute parts on one or more wind or stringed instruments (that is, single-voiced instruments such as cornets, violins, etc. which afford only a single line); and it is customary to term as organists, however, only those who are entrusted with the organ, regal and harpsichord. In Italy, musicians able to play all instruments, full-voiced as well as single-voiced, are called universal musicians; but these are seldom found, for in those parts, musicians strive to master a single instrument—or two at the most—thoroughly and try to excel other players—lest they be called Jacks of all trades and Masters of none (which is quite common among us Germans).

An Accord is an entire set of flutes, bassoons, and other instruments ranging successively from the deepest and largest instrument to the highest and smallest.

Sorts, on the other hand, refers to a single type of instrument, as is more clearly to be seen in the Universal Table following chapter IV.

Falsetto tones of flutes and other instruments are tones which skilled players are able to produce outside the natural range of wind instruments (9).

———————

of each of these there are
the following number

an Accord or Set of Instruments is comprised of various Sorts.	sets with 3 sorts	Cross Flutes	discant 2. alto, tenor 4. bass 2.	8 Cross Flutes
		Doppioni Bassanelli	discant 2. alto, tenor 3. bass 1.	6 Bassanelli
	sets with 4 sorts	Trombones	alto trombone 1. ordinary trombone 4. quart trombone 2. octave trombone 1.	8 Trombones
		Racketts Schryari	cant 2. alto, tenor 3. bass 1. large bass 1.	7 Racketts
	sets with 5 sorts	Bassoons Sordunes	discant 1. fagotto piccolo 2. chorist bassoon 3. double bn. { quart, F 1. { quint, F 1.	8 Bassoons
		Krummhorns	small discant 1. discant 2. alto, tenor 3. bass 2. large bass 1.	9 Krummhorns
		Corna Muse	discant 1. alto 1. alto, tenor 1. tenor 2. bass 1.	6 Corna Muse
	sets with 7 sorts	Bumbardes	very small shawm 1. shawm 2. small alto pommer 3. large alto pommer 2. basset or tenor pommer 2. bass pommer 2. large bass pommer 1.	13 Bumbardes and Shawms
	sets with 8 sorts	Recorders	very small exilent 2. discant, 4th lower 2. discant, 5th lower 2. alto flute 4. tenor flute 4. basset flute 4. bass flute 2. large bass flute 1.	21 Recorders

thus forming complete sets

II

Of the Pitch proper to the Organ and Other Instruments, and how the same varies in different countries and places; and further, of the difference between Choral Pitch and Chamber Pitch. Also the upper and lower pitch limitations of the human voice.

In all justness, composers and conductors as well as players ought to know how high and low wind and stringed instruments can be used, so that they will be able to compose, etc. accordingly. The composer must take great care in his compositions not to force an instrument higher than it is able to go naturally, lest the singing of the instrumental part must be resorted to, and this procedure would otherwise not be necessary.

In the same way it is also essential that every organist be able to distinguish one register of the organ from another and have knowledge of its $1^1/_2$, 2, 3 . . . 32-foot tones, so that he may adjust himself accordingly in changing the voicing.

And now although many of my readers may well have greater knowledge of these matters than I, still I wished to note down something in this respect here for the benefit and further reflection of the less practised, since such information has often been requested of me.

At the outset it is to be made clear that the pitch of organs and other musical instruments frequently varies widely. This is because in earlier times it was not the practise to play all kinds of instruments together in ensemble, and thus instrument makers built wind instruments quite differently, tuning some high and others low: for certain instruments, such as the cornet, shawm and discant violin, sound fresher and better when constructed to a higher pitch, while instruments like trombones, bassoons, bassanelli, bumbardes and bass viols sound the more grave and splendid the lower they are pitched. Thus considerable difficulty is caused the director of music when organs, positives, harpsichords and wind instruments are not tuned to the same and proper pitch.

In earlier times the choral pitch was one tone lower than now and this is still to be found on old organs and other wind instruments. But as time went on, the choral pitch was raised until it became as high as its present form in Italy, England and in the royal chapels of Germany. (However, the English tuning for instruments is somewhat lower, as may be seen from English cornets and shawms—or hoboys, as they are there called.)

There are some persons who have presumed to raise our present pitch another semitone higher. Although it is not my place to criticize this, still in my estimation, such height of pitch is found to be very uncomfortable by singers, especially altos and tenors in their upper register. Thus the choral pitch ought justly to be left as it is, for even in its present form it is often found too high—and not by singers alone, but also by players of stringed instruments like viols da braccio and viols da gamba, lutes, pandoras and the like—for only exceptional strings can bear the tension required by this high level of pitch. And due to such tension, the strings often snap back in the middle of pieces and hang by loose and useless. To keep the strings in proper tuning, then, stringed instruments ordinarily must be tuned a tone lower, and then other instruments sounding with them must similarly be played a second lower. To be sure, this procedure is difficult for inexperienced instrumentalists; but playing a second lower greatly helps the singers in the execution of their parts.

Because of all this, I am very much in favor of the distinction made in Prague and at other Catholic chapels, between choral pitch and chamber pitch. In accordance with this, the present pitch, to which almost all of our organs are now commonly tuned, is termed chamber pitch and is employed only at court dinners and other entertainments. This pitch, then, is the more convenient for players of wind and stringed instruments.

However the choral pitch, which is a whole tone lower, is employed only in church. This is done primarily for the sake of the singers, so that they can perform their parts without becoming hoarse from the highness of the range; for a very great effort is required from them in the services (especially in Catholic chapels, where there is very much singing of Psalms and the like); and further, the choral pitch is used because the human voice sounds much more pleasant in the middle and lower part of its range than when it is forced high beyond its powers and made to shriek and cry. For convenience then, and for the sake of fine suavity and sweet consent of sound, it would be advisable to tune all organs a tone lower; but it would be quite impossible to change this in our German lands, and thus we must retain the common chamber pitch (which at present is considered to be choral pitch, however, in most localities).

In England most wind instruments were formerly tuned a minor third lower than our present chamber pitch—such that the English F was the D of our chamber pitch, and their G our E. This tuning is still employed in the Netherlands. The excellent instrument maker, Johannes Bossus of Antwerp, tunes most of his harpsichords and keyboard instruments with pipes, to this same pitch.

And this would not be a bad idea, for harpsichords sound lovelier tuned to this pitch than to the chamber pitch, as every skilled instrument maker will know. Flutes and other instruments also sound better in this tuning than at the usual pitch. Their effect on the ear is quite different, since they do not sound as harsh in this low tuning.

But instruments tuned in this fashion are very inconvenient for use in full ensembles, and thus the two earlier mentioned pitches, choral and chamber pitch, must be adhered to. Nonetheless this tuning in the lower third is rather frequently employed in the Catholic chapels of Germany and in Italy. The Italians believe, and not without reason, that singing in high range is very unpleasant and without any charm, and that it causes the text to be obscured, sounding like the shrill bawling of a harvester maid. Therefore the hypoionian mode on C, when already transposed down a fifth into F, is often played a third lower—on D—on organs, positives and related instruments. Voices are better able to sing in this mode when it is transposed in this way, and it is only on this account that it is employed in this form. The hypodorian mode similarly transposed, is sung a third lower, on E. Organists and other musicians find such transpositions quite difficult. But anyone who devotes some time to practising them and does not mind the effort, will find them quite easy to master and will even take pleasure in executing them.

When the organ maker tunes an organ and all its pipes to the present common chamber tone, the lowest C of the diapason on the manual will then be the 8-foot C. This pitch will coincide with that of correctly tuned harpsichords and spinets, and is then termed Aequal by organ makers, because it conforms with the human voice throughout its compass. (More may be learned about this from the following table under column four.) This C is the lowest tone which the good court bass singer is able to produce naturally and in full voice. Some singers, however, are able to sing down to AA and GG. Although these tones are already rather unsatisfactory in quality, such singers often even attempt to reach the FF, a very imperfect tone.

Some time ago there were three bass singers (Grasser, a peasant's son, and the brothers Fischer) in the royal court of Bavaria at Munich, in the time of the famed and surpassing musician, Orlando di Lasso. (This chapel is said to have included 12 bass singers, 15 tenors, 13 altos, 16 boy singers, 5 or 6 castrati and 30 instrumentalists, making a total strength of 90 persons.) These singers were able to descend to the FF of the choral pitch and could produce it strongly and with full voice, though they could not sing higher than f, g or a. A singer named Caesaron, from Rome, has also been found to have a similar voice. Most basses can reach c' or d' in their high register, and even the f'. (Not to mention others, a monk named Neapolitanus Carolus Cassanus, who served at various electoral and royal chapels in Germany, was able to produce this tone quite purely, strongly, and in full voice, and could also descend as far as the low GG of the chamber pitch.) The ordinary basses in schools, however, can seldom sing below the E of 6-foot F with natural strength, and some are not able to rise much above a.

The approximate ranges of the voices of tenors, altos and castrati or discantists are indicated in the table following. It suffices if a tenor can reach the e', and an alto the g' of the chamber pitch. It is all the better if he can sing higher, and it will be of credit to him. But nothing definite can be concluded here about the range of voices, for the gifts of God are manifold, and one may always encounter some persons who are able to sing higher or lower than others. Nonetheless it may be stated that castrati usually have bright and full voices just as strong as those of two or three boys voices together. At the present time several extraordinary castrati are to be found in the Imperial Chapel and in the chapels of Catholic princes and electors.

And let this suffice, for the present, with regard to the pitch of instruments and of the human voice.

———————

III

Following this is a
Universal Table
of all Wind and Stringed Instruments.
therein

1. SIGNA

The clefs indicated at the beginning of every piece in order that one tone be distinguished from the other.

2. CLAVES IN SCALA TABULATURAE

The tones of the gamut according to organ tablature, and by which one may conveniently orient himself in all musical instruments. This gamut includes over six octaves; and I was unable to devise a better form for presenting it and distinguishing between its tones. I have thoroughly considered how the lowest pedal tones of from 8 to 16 feet might best be represented in symbols. It would not be unsuitable to make use of two repeated capital letters, for example, CC or DD, much as the ancients designated the higher tones of their gamut (and I have retained this here under the column, Signis); still in the end it seemed better to use heavy capital letters with a little dash below them for the lowest tones, in this fashion: C, D, etc.

3. FEET

Under column three of this table the names of tones and their size in feet are indicated according to their pitch and sound and as used by organmakers for the convenient designation of the tones and corresponding keys of pipes in all registers, such that these may readily be named and understood. And since it is essential to make these differentiations with regard to other instruments and also the human voice, and while no more appropriate word is to be found, I have had to retain the term, feet, here.

4. THE HUMAN VOICE

The essential information regarding the human voice was noted in the previous article.

_____

IV

In this table, as in the succeeding detailed articles, the following will be shown in greater detail:

1.   How the diverse kinds of each set of instruments are arranged in families.

2.   How low and high each wind instrument may be brought in its natural tone, indicated by white notes; and which high and low falsetto tones can be produced by skilled players outside the natural range of each instrument. I have indicated these falsetto tones with black notes, since, whether with instruments or voice, not everyone is able to reach them.

3.   How many strings there are on stringed instruments, and how high or low each string must be tuned with relation to one another.

4.   Together with this, it must here be made clear that throughout this entire work the instruments and tones are referred to according to chamber pitch and not in choral pitch (both clearly differentiated above); for chamber pitch is much the more commonly used and almost all instruments—both stringed and wind, and modern organs as well—are adjusted and tuned to it.

20.

UNIVERSAL TABLE (16)

VII - Recorders

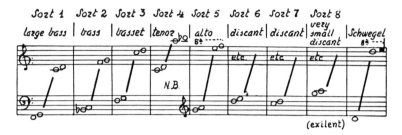

N. B. This recorder, and the cross flute in this register as well, may not only be used as a discant instrument, as which I have set it down here, but also as a tenor, an octave lower. Various musicians believe that this type of recorder and cross flute actually is a true tenor instrument in sound and that its lowest tones—the c or d in the tenor register, produce a four-foot pitch in the organ maker's measure. I, too, was actually of this opinion for a time, for with the ear it is quite difficult to perceive the true pitch; but when one compares this pitch with the sound of the organ, it is then recognized as being a true discant, with a two-foot pitch. The same holds true of the bass flute in its relation to other flutes of this kind, for the two kinds of bass flutes shown above sound just as if they were an octave lower, the lowest tone of the second sort being then taken for an 8-foot B flat or C and that of the first sort, for a 12-foot D sharp or F; but actually the pitch of the latter is no lower than six feet, and that of the other, just four feet.

22.

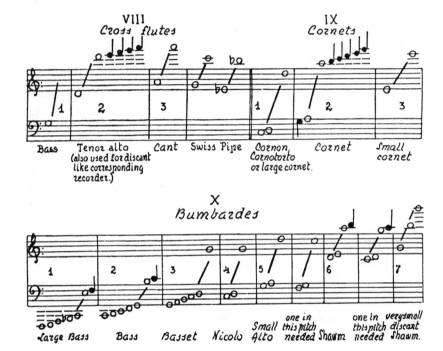

VIII
Cross flutes

1
Bass

2
Tenor alto
(also used for discant
like corresponding
recorder.)

3
Cant

Swiss Pipe

IX
Cornets

1
Cornon,
Cornotorto
or large cornet.

2
Cornet

3
Small
cornet

X
Bumbardes

1
Large Bass

2
Bass

3
Basset

4
Nicolo

5
Alto

one in
Small this pitch
needed Shawm

6

one in very small
this pitch discant
needed Shawm.

7

XI
Bassoons · Dulcians

XII
Sordunes

XIII
Doppioni

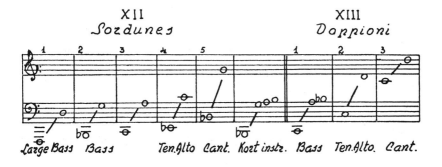

24.

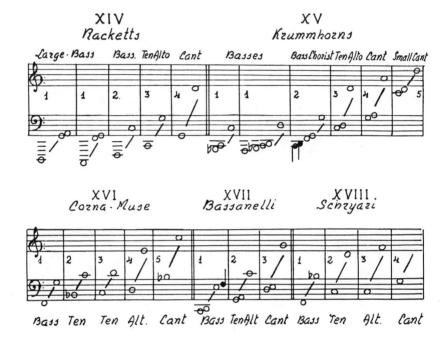

25.

XIX
Bagpipes

Large Bock Chaunter   Bock Shepherds Pipe   *Hümmelchen*   *Dudey*

chaunters   chaunters   chaunters

XX
Viols da Gamba

Very Large
Contrabass
Viol da Gamba   Large Bass   Small Bass   Tenor Alto   *Violette picciola*   or Cant

a   b   c   a   b   c   d   e   a b c d e   a b c d e

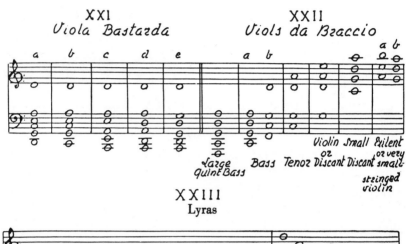

XXI
Viola Bastarda

XXII
Viols da Braccio

a   b   c   d   e   a   b   a b

Violin Small Silent
Large   Bass Tenor Discant Discant or very
Quint Bass   small
                                    stringed
                                    violin

XXIII
Lyras

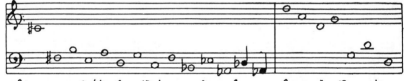

Lirone perfetto, Arce Violya, or Large Lyra   Lyra da Braccio

X X I V
Lute

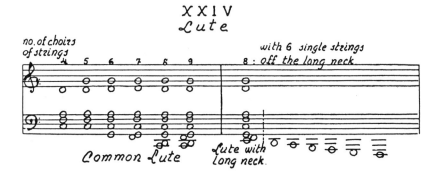

Common Lute

Lute with long neck.

X X V
Theorboes

1.- Roman   2.- Paduan

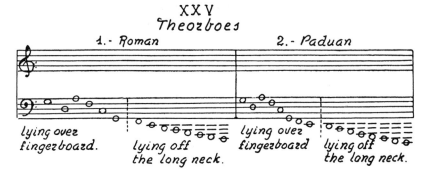

lying over fingerboard.

lying off the long neck.

lying over fingerboard

lying off the long neck.

XXVI
Quintern

XXVII
Mandürchen

XXVIII
Banduz

XXIX
Penorcon

XXX
Orpheoreon

XXXI
Cithers

French

Common Italian

Five-choired

Old. Italian

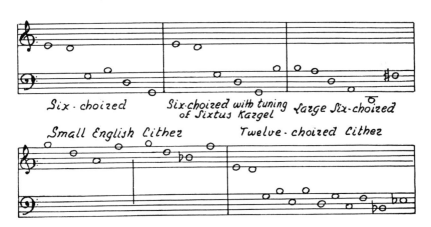

Six - choired Cither

Six - choired   Six-choired with tuning   Large Six-choired
              of Sixtus Kargel

Small English Cither   Twelve - choired Cither

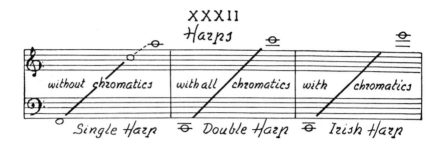

XXXII

Harps

without chromatics | with all chromatics | with chromatics

Single Harp   Double Harp   Irish Harp

It will not be necessary to enter into this table the remaining instruments treated in chapters 33, 34, 35, 36 etc. since ample report on them may there be found.

Since at the end of the First Part of this Second Volume I have divided instruments into Inflatilia and Fidicinia, or wind and stringed instruments, there will follow here

firstly

Wind Instruments

in Italian

Instrumenta da Fiato

V
Tromboni, Trombones
(Theatre of Instruments, Plate VIII)

Of the trombone (in Latin, tuba ductilis, oblonga; in Italian, trombone, trombetta) there are four kinds or sorts.

1.   The Alto or Discant trombone (trombino, trombetta picciola), on which a discant can be played naturally and well. However, because of its small body, it does not sound as well as the high register of the ordinary trombone, when this height is achieved on the latter with good embouchure.

2.   The ordinary trombone (tuba minor, trombetta or trombone piccolo) can be played up to f' and down to E in natural tones and with good embouchure can be brought lower, and also a couple tones higher, thus serving quite well for alto parts.

Some players (among them the famed master, Phileno, of Munich) command this instrument so well that they are able to sound the low D and the high c", d" and e" without any difficulty. I heard another player at Dresden—Erhardus Borussus, who is said to be living in Poland at present. He mastered this instrument to such a high degree that he could play almost as high as a cornet—that is, to the high g" sol re ut—and as low as a quart-trombone, or to the AA; and was able to execute rapid coloraturas and jumps on his instrument just as is done on the viola bastarda and cornet. This is to be seen at the end of the fourth part of the Third Volume.

3.   The Quart-Trombone (tuba major, trombone major, trombone grande, trombone majore) of which some are a fourth and others a fifth lower than the ordinary trombone, and an octave below the alto trombone. One who plays the ordinary trombone with facility will also make easy progress with this instrument if he just imagines everything that he is to play to be a fifth higher, as if the tenor clef were indicated instead of the bass clef:

This instrument could justly be called a Quint-Trombone. It must also be noted here that because quart-trombones differ in size, their slide positions do not coincide.

4.   The Octave Trombone (tuba maxima, trombone doppio; trombone alla ottava bassa) was seldom found before modern times, and of these instruments I know two kinds. The one is exactly twice as long as the ordinary trombone without crooks and therefore entirely coincides with it in slide-lengths, etc; but its pitch is an octave lower, extending to the E in natural tone, and in falsetto, with good embouchure, to the D and C. This kind of octave trombone was made four years ago by a musician named Hans Schreiber. See drawing on plates VI and VII (8).

The other kind is not quite twice as long as the common trombone, but its depth is brought about by its rather wider tubes and also by the use of crooks. Octave trombones of this kind were already in use many years ago at various chapels. Before all other wind instruments, the trombone is especially good for use in all kinds of combinations and ensembles, for it can be made to produce every tone a little sharp or flat. This is accomplished not only by the attaching or removal of crooks (crommettes) or other detachable tube sections (polettes), but also just with the lips and breath; for a skilled trombone player is able to modify the pitch of every chromatic tone of the range by means of his embouchure and mouthpiece, and without making use of crooks. This cannot be brought about on instruments with finger holes.

VI
The Trumpet
(plate VIII)

The trumpet (in Vulgar Latin, taratantara; or tuba—instrumentum in curvum ex aere argentove, cujus sonitu milites, equique, ad praelium inflammantur: a tubis id est, canalis concavitate nomen habens; and in Italian, tromba) is a magnificent instrument. It is remarkable that in its higher register this instrument affords conjunctly almost all the diatonic tones, and various chromatic tones as well. This makes possible the playing of all kinds of melodies on it and without the use of slides, by which trombones are regulated. Earlier the trumpet was built to the fundamental tone, D, in the chamber pitch. Field trumpets have retained this tuning.

But a short time ago it became the practise in many court orchestras either to use the trumpet in a lengthened form or to attach crook tubes to its front, such that the fundamental tone of the instrument was brought a tone lower, to the C ad modum hypoionicum—the tuning then being at the choral pitch. Of this Glareanus writes the following in Book Two, chap. 27 of his "Dodecachordon": "Tubarum sonitus hodie inter Modi Hypoionici limites constat, integra omnibus Chordis diapente, sed diatessaron extremis potissimum."

Some people favor tuning trumpets still a half tone or a whole tone lower, on B flat.

Some persons prefer trumpets fashioned in the form of a post-horn and wound round like a snake. But such trumpets are not as good in tone as the other trumpets. One also encounters very long trumpets built from bast. In our towns we often see shepherds from the Voigtland and Switzerland seeking their meals by playing these long instruments. (Drawings of all these are found on plate VIII.)

VII

Flutes and Recorders

(plate IX)

All recorders (Latin, fistula; Italian, flauto) have seven holes in front and one in back. The two adjacent holes found at the lower end of the instrument both produce the same pitch. They are arranged in this double form only because some musicians play with the left hand below and others with the right. Thus one of these holes must be plugged with wax.

The largest recorders do not ordinarily produce more than thirteen tones, but the small ones, if good, afford fourteen. In exceptional cases, however, skilled players are able to obtain four tones above that and even the seventh tone above the mentioned thirteen or fourteen. These tones are called falsetto tones, as indicated in the first chapter.

The foregoing table actually shows how many sorts there are of recorders and other instruments treated in this work. Nevertheless, for the sake of further information I wish to note down the eight sorts of recorders here.

1. the small flute . . . two octaves higher than the cornet
2. the discant flute . . . a fourth lower than the small flute
3. the discant flute . . . a fifth lower than the small flute
4. the alto flute . . . . an octave lower than the small flute
5. the tenor flute . . . . a fifth lower than the alto flute
6. the basset flute . . . another fifth lower
   (with a key or fontanelle below)
7. the bass flute . . . . a fifth lower than the basset flute
8. the large flute . . . . an octave lower than the basset.

A complete set such as this can be procured in Venice for about eighty thaler. Here should also be mentioned the Schwegel, also called Stamentien-pipe. It has only two holes on the front bottom and one in back. It is similar in length to the transverse flute, but is blown like a recorder. The English use it together with a drum and play it with the left hand. (plate IX) It goes in range from d' up to d''', e''' and even further. Some are a fifth lower, from to g'' or a''. It is remarkable that with but three holes this instrument affords the same extent of range as instruments with six or seven holes.

Then there are also very small recorders about three or four inches long and with three holes in front and one in back. These similarly afford almost two octaves. (plate IX). Both the Schwegel and these very small recorders must be supported at the end by the fifth finger. The Stamentien-pipe is twenty inches long, its tenor, 26, and bass, 30.

I must also mention that not a little difficulty is involved in setting up a flute ensemble (in Italian, choro da flauto: see Volume Three for further explanation); for it is seldom that one finds flutes which are correctly in tune with one another. This is because like church organs they are easily affected by heat and cold, their pitch being found lower in winter and higher in summer. Thus it would be advisable to have two full sets of wind instruments at hand, the instruments of one set being built to a pitch half a semitone below the pitch of those of the other set. But it occurred to me to piece apart the flutes half way between the mouthpiece and the highest finger hole, thus lengthening the upper section of the pipe by the breadth of two fingers. This makes the length of the tube variable and thus its pitch may be accordingly adjusted higher or lower. Although certain reputed instrument makers were of the opinion that this would make some of the tones of the flute false, they actually had no objections to the idea—apart from the fact that certain of the highest tones did not respond very well.

This has similarly been attempted successfully on bassanelli (see chap. XVII). The same device is used on the cornet, its mouthpiece being set further in or out.

VIII
Cross Flutes
(plate IX)

The Cross Flute (Italian, traversa or fiffaro) has six holes in front and none in back. It produces fifteen natural tones and four falsetto tones besides, thus nineteen in all, just as the cornet.

This is also the case with the Dulceflute (also called a cross flute) except that it has eight holes like the recorder.

To be included here is also the Swiss Pipe or Field Pipe. It has its own special fingerings (10) which do not entirely coincide with those of the cross flute, and is only used together with drums. (plate XXIII).

IX
Cornets
(plate VIII)

Cornets (Italian, cornetti; and perhaps the same as the buccina or cornua of the Romans) are of two kinds, Recti and Curvi, or straight and curved. Of the straight cornets there are again two kinds:

1.   the Cornetto Diritto, a straight cornet to which a separate mouthpiece must be attached.

2.   the Cornetto Muto, a straight cornet the mouthpiece of which is undetachable, having been lathed on the instrument. These instruments are quite soft and quiet in tone and lovely to listen to. Thus they are called "stille Zincken". (plate XIII)

3.   the Cornetti Curvi are black curved cornets.

All cornets without distinction, produce fifteen natural tones, from a to a". With falsetto tones some can reach the high e"' and occasionally even the high g"' quite well, and also the low g and f.

4.   the Corno or Cornetto Torto, also called Cornon, is a large cornet almost in the shape of an S, and is a fifth lower than the ordinary cornet. Although it is maintained by some that this instrument produces only eleven natural tones and has no falsetto above that, this is not actually the case; for like the common cornet, fifteen tones may be had on it. But since its tone is quite unlovely and hornlike, I consider it better to use a trombone in its stead.

5.   Yet to be mentioned is the Cornettino, a very small cornet a fifth higher than the common cornet, and not unpleasing to hear.

X

Pommers, Bombardoni or Bumbardes, and Shawms
(plate XI)

Bombyces, sive Bombi Graecis etiam vocari queunt longae tibiae, quae difficulter magnaque; cum contentione flatus impulsae sonum crassiorem edunt.

Bumbardes (in Italian, bombardo or bombardone; French, hautbois; English, hoboy) take their name without a doubt from "a bombo", that is, humming, and are all, both large and small, designated by the term bumbarde or pommer. In Italian the large bass bumbarde is called bombardone, and the ordinary bass, bombardo. The tenor has four low metal keys with which it can be brought down to the G of the bass; thus a bass part can if necessary be played by it. For this reason it is called a basset. Following it is the Nicolo, the same as the basset in size and register; but this instrument has only one key and thus can be brought no lower than the c of the tenor. (plate XIII). The alto bumbarde is called the bombardo piccolo. It is almost the same as the shawm in size, but has one key and is a fifth lower in pitch. Only the highest discant of these instruments is called Shawm (Italian, piffaro; Latin, gingrina, because it sounds just like the cackling of a goose—from gingrire, to cackle). The shawm has no keys.

Most shawms are pitched a tone higher than the corresponding cornets and trombones.

Since early times, and still today, most wind instruments such as flutes, shawms and krummhorns, were constructed to tunings a fifth apart from one another within their proper sets. As I have noted in the foregoing table, this is so that instruments of the same set can be employed in groups of threes, one instrument being used for the bass part, the second for the tenor or alto (for tenor and alto parts can always be played by instruments similar in sound and construction) and the third, then, for the cantus. But when a fourth kind is to be added, the composition must be transposed a fourth lower—in the hypoionian mode, for instance, from c' to g (and not from c' to f!) thus making a Cantus Fictus out of the piece. Or if the piece is already in f, it must then be transposed a tone higher; and this works out quite well, particularly for bumbardes and shawms. But if it is desired to add a fifth instrument above or below, it becomes very difficult to match them all together in intonation; for the outermost instruments of the set are then separated by five fifths or the interval of a seventeenth, which amounts to the same as a ditonus or major third—a relationship very difficult to account for. But even this combination may yield workable results provided the music is arranged accordingly and the intonation handled carefully. Still, the makers of instruments might well be advised to construct another kind of discant (and also tenor) a tone lower, that is, a fourth above the next lower instrument of its set, rather than the usual fifth. On this basis even five-part settings can be played well, since the outermost parts will be correctly in tune—as is recognized by some people, few though they may be.

XI

Bassoons, Dulcians

(plate X)

Bassoons and Dulcians (Italian, fagotto or dolcesuono) are generally so named without differentiation. However, some persons believe the true dulcian to be the instrument which the English call the Zingol Korthol. In their lower range and in tone, dulcians are similar to the basset bumbarde, though still quieter and softer; and perhaps it is from this loveliness of sound that they are called dulcians—from dulcisonantes, or sweetly sounding. For while the tube of bumbardes is straight and is open at the bottom, that of bassoons is bent double, such that the bell is at the top. Sometimes this bell has a punctured cover (as I will mention in Part Four in connection with certain reed stops on the organ). This makes the tone much less strong, and considerably softer and lovelier. For the same reasons the open diapason and trombone stops of the organ sound much stronger and fresher than covered reed stops.

On the Chorist bassoon, the lowest key is C, and on the Double bassoon, *F*. There are two kinds of double bassoons, the Quint bassoon, which reaches the low *F* of the large bass bumbarde; and the Quart bassoon, which can only be brought down to the *G* (plate VII). The latter is the more suitable for playing melodies with raised tones, and the former, for those with flattened tones. It is best when both these kinds of double bassoons are available in an ensemble, for chromatic tones cannot be produced as conveniently by means of keys as with uncovered finger holes.

At present the master who constructed the octave trombones is now at work building a large contrabassoon, to be a fourth below the double bassoon and thus an octave below the chorist bassoon, and which will afford the 16-foot C. If he should succeed in this, he will indeed have produced a unique and remarkable instrument; for even on the organ it is often difficult to construct the two lowest tones of the large trombone stops—the 16-foot C and D, to sound quite pure. But time will tell.

XII

Sordunes

(plate XII)

Sordunes (Italian, sordoni, and called dulcians by some) are almost the same as the corna muse and krummhorn in tone. Although the lowest bass sordune is hardly half so long as the double bassoon, it nevertheless can be brought just as low in pitch. This is quite remarkable, for its tube-length, as in bassoons, is but once doubled back on itself. Lodovico Zacconi calls these instruments sordoni. Sordunes have twelve visible holes—and some have two keys as well, making fourteen holes. Besides these there is a hole below for moisture and one on top from which the sound issues. The largest sordune is 2 feet 5 inches long. But then I have seen a sordune in length and shape quite the same as one of these, but no lower than the tenor in pitch. It was called a Kort Instrument. I have not yet been able to think of the reason for this difference, nor have I received any information about it from others.

XIII

Doppioni

The mentioned Zacconi refers to similar instruments which he calls Doppioni. In spite of my efforts, I have not yet been able to examine such an instrument. It is perhaps like number 7 on plate XII, or similar to the sordune or corna muse—as may well be supposed from its pitch and varieties, shown in the table.

XIV

Racketts

(plate X)

Racketts are quite short instruments, as may be seen from plate X, where they can be measured. Yet because their inside tubing is coiled around nine times, this amounts to the same as if the body were nine times as long as it actually is. Thus racketts produce a low sound like the largest bumbarde or double bassoon. Some bass racketts may be found pitched a semitone or a minor third lower still, such that they afford the $\overline{D}$, thus having a 15-foot pitch. I myself designed and recently had constructed a rackett which can be brought down to the 16-foot C, and which in its lower register is similar to the largest diapason stops of the organ. Its body is no more than eleven inches in length. Racketts have quite a few holes, but never more than eleven. These instruments rarely afford falsetto tones, since they do not give tones beyond those yielded by the holes themselves. However, if a rackett is well bored and is played by a good player, it then can be made to yield a few more tones. In sound racketts are quite soft, almost as if one were blowing through a comb. They have no particular grace when a whole set of them is used together; but when viols da gamba are used with them, or when a single rackett is used together with other wind or stringed instruments and a harpsichord or the like, and is played by a good musician, it is indeed a lovely instrument. It is particularly pleasing and fine to hear on bass parts.

In general, sordunes, kort instruments, racketts, corna muse, krummhorns and schryari do not yield any tones beyond those given by their holes. But bumbardes, shawms, bassoons, dulcians and bassanelli can all be brought several tones higher (as the foregoing table shows) without overblowing.

XV
Krummhorns
(plate XIII)

Krummhorns (Latin, lituus; Italian, storti or cornamuti torti) are not blown by direct contact with a reed, but as on corna muse, schryari and bagpipes, their reed is encased in a separate capsule. Therefore one can not directly control them and is not able to influence them in pitch. Krummhorns have one hole in back and six in front, and in addition to these, two more holes at the bottom which reach another two or three lower tones. But since these holes can not be reached directly with the fingers, special keys, often of brass, are necessary for them.

These two lowermost holes must be kept open anyway, else the instrument would not be correctly in tune and the seventh hole below would bring the pitch of the instrument lower than it rightly ought to be.

According to this principle, the organ maker must often correct large and small reed stops to the proper pitch by means of holes when these stops do not respond correctly. (Still, this procedure is not very commendable.) Krummhorns yield no pitches beyond those given by their holes and keys, as was previously mentioned.

XVI
Corna Muse
(plate VII)

Corna Muse are straight like bassanelli. They are covered below, and around the bell have several little holes, from which the sound issues. In sound they are quite similar to krummhorns, but quieter, lovelier and very soft. Thus they might justly be named still, soft krummhorns, much as the cornetti muti could be called soft cornets. They have no keys at all, and sound at the chorus pitch, that is, a tone lower than the true chamber pitch.

XVII
Bassanelli
(plate XII)

Bassanelli take their name from the master who invented them, Johann Bassano, a distinguished instrumentalist and composer at Venice. The tubing of bassanelli is straight and opens at the bottom; and these instruments have just one brass key. They are blown by direct contact with reeds, just as are bassoons, bumbardes and bassets, and in tone are almost the same as these instruments, though much softer. The Cant, which is the smallest of the bassanelli, is particularly fine to hear on the tenor part in ensembles in which all kinds and sets of instruments are used, for it is quite accurate in pitch, and is similar to flutes in the rendering of a tenor part. With good reeds, bassanelli can be brought quite high. Like shawms, they have seven holes, with a key on the lowest. In back, however, no hole is to be found. They are a fourth lower than the chamber pitch, for their lowest key in the bass is F; but in the chamber pitch this is reckoned as the 8-foot C.

XVIII
Schryari
(plate XII)

Schryari (in German, Schreierpfeiffen) are strong and fresh in tone and can be used alone, or together with other instruments. They have holes in back as well as in front, and are almost the same as the corna muse in length and shape; but because they are open at the bottom, are much stronger in sound. The discant, however, is covered below, but has many holes near the covering through which the wind can escape. Schryari do not yield pitches beyond those brought by their holes.

XIX
Bagpipes
(plates V, XI, XIII)

Of bagpipes (Latin, tibia utricularis; Italian, corna musa) there are many kinds:

1. the Bock, which has just one long chaunter tube, on the deep C. Some are a fourth deeper, on GG, and are rightly called large bocks.

2. the Shepherds Pipe, which has two drones on b flat and f. Shepherds pipes are usually out of tune in the upper holes. I believe this is because they have no thumb holes in back. But other bagpipes, such as the Bock, Hümmelchen and Dudey, have a hole in back such that their tuning may better be regulated.

3. the Hümmelchen, which also has only two drones on f' and c'.

4. the Dudey, however, has three small drones, on e' flat, b' flat and e'' flat.

In the archbishopric of Magdeburg I saw a special kind of bagpipe somewhat larger than the shepherds pipe and a third lower. It had two chaunters, and below had two small drones as well, one for the left hand and the other for the right. On each of these latter there were three holes in front and one in back, for the thumb, such that g, a', b', c' and d' could be played with the left hand, and d', e' f', g' and a' with the right. Thus bicinia (12) could be played on it quite easily. A drawing of it is to be found on plate V.

In France a little bagpipe or Hümmelchen (plate XIII) has been constructed into which air is pumped by means of a small bellows operated by one arm alone.

An inventor, mentioned earlier in article V, gave this matter much thought and fashioned an entire set of five of these bagpipes controlled with bellows, such that a piece for four or five voices could be played by them. But I do not find the sound of such a combination very pleasing.

The Regal (plate IV) (which belongs in a sense here together with the wind instruments—since it is operated by air) will be treated later, in chapter 43 (11), after the string instruments and shortly before the article on organs. A drawing of it is found on plate IV.

FIDICINIA INSTRUMENTA

or

STRINGED INSTRUMENTS

XX

Viols and Violins

There are two kinds of viols and violins, the viols da gamba and the viols da braccio, or da brazzo. The viol da gamba is so called because it is held between the two legs, gamba being the Italian term for leg: le gambe, the legs. Because the viols da gamba are much the larger and have longer necks and strings, they produce a far lovelier sound than the viols da braccio, held on the arm. Musicians differentiate between these two types of instruments by calling the viols da gamba simply viols and the viols da braccio, violins—or Polish fiddles, perhaps because they are supposed to have originated in Poland, or else while the best players of these instruments are found there.

The viols da gamba have six strings tuned in fourths and with a third in the middle, as on six-choired lutes. The English, when they play with viols alone, tune everything a fourth or fifth lower, such that although the lowest string of the small bass is thought of as D, that of the tenor-alto as A, and of the Cantus as e, each of them is actually tuned a fifth lower than these pitches, namely, the bass to G, the alto-tenor to D and the discant to A in the chamber pitch—as is shown on the table. In a set of these instruments, this low tuning brings about a much more pleasant, splendid and magnificent sound than that produced when they are kept at the ordinary pitch level (plate XX).

The large viol da gamba (Italian, violone or contrabasso da gamba, with drawing on plate VI) is usually tuned in fourths throughout, and this, in my estimation, is good. I do not consider it very important how each player tunes his violin or viol so long as he is able to execute his part correctly and well.

Some persons get special notions about such things, and are wont to scorn organists who do not make use of this or that way of fingering. But this, I believe, is not even worthy of discussion. Let one run up and down the keyboard with the front, middle or rear fingers and even with his nose if it helps, for so long as what he plays sounds fine and pure and is correct and pleasant to the ear, it is not very important by what means he accomplishes it.

N. B. For all these bowed instruments spanned with gut strings, the notes in the foregoing table indicate only how high or low each string may be tuned, and not how high one can ascend on them with fingers and frets—and this is common knowledge.

Earlier these viols da gamba were strung in three ways, as is to be found in Agricola; for some had three, some four, and some (as in plate XX) five strings, as many be seen in the foregoing Universal Table.

Since the thinnest strings of the large bass gamba or violone seldom bear great tension well, due to the large space between the upper saddle and the bridge, a musician in Prague, after considering this matter earnestly, designed and produced a bass violin with six strings, each a little shorter than the next, such that the thinnest string is almost a foot—that is, 12 inches—shorter than the largest. He constructed the lower saddle (as on penorcons and orpheoreons) in an upward slanting position, the upper saddle being made to slant downward; and thus the spacing of the frets was quite uneven and these were impossible for the fingers to play on. Because of this, the following means was contrived by which the frets could be contacted in the proper place on each string: a covering was made over the entire neck of the instrument, as on the peasants lyra (4), and along the lower edge of this cover are set six rows of wooden keys with five keys in each row; and these are depressed just as are the keys of the peasants lyra.

To these keys were fastened strong brass wires, as on the brass keys of large pommers. Each of these was just long enough to reach its corresponding fret. This is quite a fine device, for each string can thus maintain its own tension, and the bass player does not have to move around so much with his hand, since all the keys are close together.

But pegs of iron, rather than of wood, are used at the top of the neck; and these pegs are notched, such that their position is controlled by a feather cog much as watch movement is controlled. And what displeases me is that when a peg is pulled up or let down by a single notch, the corresponding string sharpens or flattens in such a way that its deviation from the correct pitch may amount to as much as two commata. Thus in my estimation the instrument cannot be made to combine with other instruments satisfactorily and with accurate tuning.

But this could easily be corrected if the notches of these pegs were to be cut as close as possible to one another such that the raising or lowering of a peg by a single notch would not incur this discrepancy of pitch in so marked a form. Thus the strings could be tuned more purely and accurately with other instruments. Pegs in this form are much better and more sturdy than the ordinary kind of peg, since they do not loosen or give way.

N B

Recently two very large double-bass gambas (plate V) were constructed. In combination with these instruments, bass gambas can be used on tenor and alto parts of a piece, and the small bass viol da gamba on the discant. I have composed a piece, "Lauda Hierusalem Dominum", for this and other combinations, and it will appear shortly, with the help of God, in my "Polyhymnia Nona". In it the five voices of this combination must all be played an octave lower. But then because the instruments really mumble and grumble too much together in such a combination—just as on the organ when one plays deep thirds and fifths on the manual together with the low diapason and 16-foot covered flute—I have found that it is much more acceptable and pleasant to use the usual gambas on the upper and middle parts and in the proper octave, with the large double-bass gamba on the bass part and sounding an octave lower than written. In this way the double-bass gamba, when heard from a distance, sounds like the deep sub-bass of an organ.

And I must also mention that when it is desired to play a part on one of these large double-bass gambas or on the octave trombone, the bass must be rewritten with the F-clef on the middle line of the staff and the lowest notes must all be written an octave higher, like a low tenor. In this way it is quite easy for the player and is just as if he were playing his part on a tenor instrument—for low instruments like these are an octave below the proper tenor range.

This can also be made use of now and then for double bassoons and large bass pommers.

XXI

Viola Bastarda

(plate XX)

This is a kind of viol da gamba. It is tuned the same as the tenor gamba, which can be used in its place if necessary. But its body is somewhat longer and larger than that of the tenor. It is possible that the viola bastarda received its name from the fact that it affords a mixture of all parts, for it is not restricted to any one part and a good player is able to execute on it madrigals, or whatever else he wishes to play, in skillfully carrying the imitations and harmonies through all possible voices —now above in the discant, now below in the bass, and now in the middle on the tenor and alto; and embellishing them with leaps and ornamentations and so treating the piece that all its voices can quite clearly be heard in their imitations and cadences. I wanted at first to include two or three examples of this at the end of this third part for the benefit of those to whom it is unfamiliar; but have decided to save it for the appendix of the Third Volume, namely under "Introductio pro Symphoniacis".

The viola bastarda is tuned in various manners, as may be seen from the table, and in other ways besides, depending on how a piece has been set and arranged.

Something quite unusual has been devised for this instrument in England. Below the usual six strings, eight more steel or wound brass strings are spanned over a brass bridge, like those used on pandoras. These strings must be exactly and justly tuned together with the upper set of strings. Now, when one of the upper gut strings is touched by the finger or by a bow, the brass or steel strings of the lower rank resonate along with it with a sympathetic shaking and quivering, such that the loveliness of the harmony is increased and heightened.

Thus it is clearly and obviously to be seen that the harmony of consonances is based entirely on Nature. This is demonstrated when a viol string is made to sound in a room in which a lute or cither may be found hanging on a wall or lying on a table; for then any of the lute or cither strings which is tuned exactly the same as the sounded viol string, will respond in sound. This can be observed even more clearly when a small blade of straw is set on the same lute or cither string.

Brass and steel strings react to this much more sensitively than gut strings, for they both swing into motion and resonate together with the other strings. On the bass viol da gamba it frequently happens that when the low G is sharply stroked by the bow, a higher string tuned to the octave of the G is also set into motion and resonates along with it. And then further, when an organ maker is setting up a new organ and tuning and setting into place its pipes one after the other, if he should want quickly to locate the particular pipe among them which he needs, he simply sounds on the organ the pipe tuned an octave lower than the needed one. Then by touching the pipes one after another, he is readily able to recognize the required pipe by its shaking: for it is set to quivering by the sound and pitch of the one played on the organ, such that its motion can actually be felt.

XXII

the Viol da Braccio

(plate XXI)

The Viol da Braccio, or Violino da Brazzo, is also called Violin and is named Fiddle by the common folk. It is named da braccio because it is held on the arm.

The bass, tenor and discant of this instrument (the last of which is also called violino, violetta picciola and rebecchino) all have four strings, and the very small violin (called pochette in French—see plate XVI) has three. All these strings are tuned in fifths. Since everyone is familiar with these instruments it is unnecessary to deal further with them here. When brass and steel strings are used on these instruments they produce a softer and lovelier tone than with other strings.

The various kinds of these instruments are to be found on plate XXI and also in the foregoing table.

XXIII

the Lyra

(plate XVII)

The peasant lyra and the lyras of street women, instruments which are ground with one hand while the keys are fingered by the left hand, will not be treated here. (Drawings of them are to be seen in plate XXII.)

There are two kinds of the Italian Lyra:

1. the Large Lyra (lirone perfetto, arce violyra; or as the above mentioned Ludovico Zacconi names it, arce-viola telire. See drawing on plate XVII). In structure it is like the bass viol da gamba, but has a somewhat wider body and broader neck due to the large number of strings. Some large lyras have twelve, some fourteen strings; and others have another two off the neck, making sixteen. Madrigals and other compositions, both chromatic as well as diatonic, can be played on these, and a fine harmonious sound is produced. But still now and then the highest or the lowest voice must be left out (as is the case with the small cither) and on this account a bass or discant may well be used together with it.

2. The Small Lyra is like the tenor viol da braccio, and is called Lyra da Braccio. It has seven strings, two of them off the fingerboard and the other five lying on it. Tricinia (12) and other pieces can be played on it, almost like a cither. See drawing on plate XX.

XXIV

the Testudo or Lute

(plate XVI)

The Lute (Latin, testudo or chelys; Italian, liuto) had only four choirs of doubled strings originally—namely c f a d' like the quintern; but later another pair of strings was made for it, resulting in c f a d' g'.

50.

The strings of the lute are differently named and reckoned in different countries, such that the:

g', d', a, f, c, (G) is called

in Italy and France
- canto; soprano; la chanterelle
- terzo
- quarto
- quinto; la basse contre

in England (13) and the Netherlands
- prime (treble)
- secunde
- tertie
- quarte
- quinte

in Germany
- quint
- quart
- terz
- secund
- prim

earlier in Germany
- Quintsaite
- Kleinsaite
- Grosssangsaite
- Klein Brummer
- Mittel Brummer
- Gross Brummer

Then besides these strings, a sixth string was added below, on Gamma ut (G); and further, a seventh, on F fa ut. As time went on even more were added until presently eight, nine and sometimes even ten, eleven and more choirs of strings are used.

It is not necessary to indicate here how the seventh, eighth and ninth choirs of strings are tuned, since each player adjusts them as he pleases, according to his habitude or to the requirements of the pieces he wishes to play.

Nowadays the lute generally has a long neck, almost as on theorboes. Eight or seven choirs of double strings lie over the fretted fingerboard of the lute, and outside, along the fingerboard, six single strings are fixed on to the upper head of the long theorbo-neck. These serve to reinforce the bass, making it sound quite brilliant. There is no particular difference between this lute and the theorbo, except that on the lute, double strings are found over the fretted fingerboard, while on the theorbo single strings are used throughout and the low fourth and fifth strings must be tuned an octave lower.

How to set up an ensemble of lutes of different sizes.

When it is desired to tune several different lutes together, their various treble strings must be tuned as follows:

1. small octave lute   d' or c'
2. small discant lute   b'
3. discant lute   a'
4. usual choir or alto lute   g'
5. tenor lute   c'
6. bass lute   d
7. large octave bass lute   g

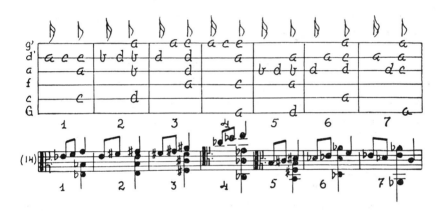

Though, to be sure, every part of the lute is named and pronounced differently by different persons, I favor the following nomenclature: (13)

the lowermost round part or belly . . . . the Corpus or body
the part facing upwards . . . . Dach or roof
the parts over which the strings are spanned:
    lower . . . . Hals or neck
    upper . . . . Griff or fingerboard
the part into which the pegs are set . . . . Theorbenkragen or
                                                 theorbo-collar
the neck extension recently added . . . . Theorbenhals or
                                                 theorbo-neck

XXV

the Theorbo

(plates V and XVI)

The Theorbo is not unlike the large bass lute, but has more strings —namely fourteen or sixteen—and has an additional neck extending above the usual fretted fingerboard. Like the viola bastarda the theorbo is used as an accompanying instrument for sopranos and tenors, for no coloraturas and ornamentations can be executed on it because of its size and wide fretting; and thus a quite simple finger technique must be used on it (17). The theorbo is also very lovely to hear together with other instruments in full ensemble and whenever else it is used together with bass instruments or in their stead.

There are two varieties of theorboes, the one with gut strings and the other with brass and steel strings. Some musicians now fit out the common lute with metal strings; but when this is done, the low fourth and fifth choirs of strings are tuned an octave lower than usual, as is the case with the theorbo. Due to the length of the body of the theorbo, this low tuning is necessary when metal strings are used, for such strings do not afford the proper tension for the higher pitches.

The theorboes made in Rome, called Chitarrone, have a very long neck, such that the entire length of the instrument amounts to $6^{1}/_{2}$ feet 2 inches. Their body is not as wide and awkward to hold and play as are the instruments made up to the present in Padua and measuring only 5 feet in length. On Roman theorboes (now also being made by Martin Schott in Prague—see plate V) the fretted fingerboard has only six strings spanned over it, while on the Paduan instruments there are eight. In addition to these strings, on both types of theorbo eight other strings lie alongside the higher extension of neck. But since constant changes take place in these various matters, nothing very definitive may be stated about them here.

———————

XXVI
the Quintern
(plate XVI)

The Quintern or Chiterna is an instrument with four choirs of strings tuned like the very earliest lutes (treated in chapter XXIV). It does not have a round belly, but like a pandora is quite flat, and hardly two or three fingers in width. A drawing of it may be found on plate XVI.

Some quinterns have five pairs of strings, and in Italy the charlatans and saltimbanco (who are like our comedians and buffoons) strum on these in singing their villanelle and other crude songs.

But none the less the quintern can be used by good singers for accompanying pleasing and lovely songs.

XXVII
Pandurina or Mandürchen
(plate XVI)

The Pandurina is variously named Bandürchen, Mandur or Mandurinchen (because it is easy to master and play). It is like a quite small lute with four strings, and is tuned to g d' g' d''. Some pandurinas have five pairs of strings and can easily be carried inside a coat. In France these instruments are said to be very common, and some musicians are so skilled on them that they can play courantes, voltes and other French dances and songs of the like, and also passamezzi, fugues and fantasias, employing a feather quill as with the cither, or else using just a single finger and playing rapidly, evenly and purely just as if three or four fingers were being used. Some musicians do use two or more fingers in playing it, according to their practise.

XXVIII
Pandora or Bandur
(plate XVII)

The Bandur (fortasse simile quid, si non idem fuit πανδοῦρα sive πανδωρὶς Graecorum) was devised in England after the fashion of the lute, and is rather like a large cither. It has single, double or also fourfold or more wound brass and steel strings and like a lute is variously tuned in six and sometimes seven choirs of strings. Low fifth strings are not made use of on this instrument, as is the case on the lute.

XXIX
Penorcon
(plate XVII)

The Penorcon is an instrument of almost the same kind, only its body is a little broader than that of the bandur, and its fingerboard is quite broad, so that nine choirs of strings can be strung over it. In length it is somewhat shorter than the bandur and longer than an orpheoreon.

XXX
Orpheoreon
(plate XVII)

The Orpheoreon is like the bandur in shape, though somewhat smaller. It has brass and steel strings and is tuned to chamber pitch like the lute, with the treble strings on g'.

XXXI
Cithara
(plate XVI)

The Cithara, a cither, is today quite a different musical instrument from that of the ancients, whose cithara was like our present harp, as may be seen from chapter XXIII following.

There are five kinds of cithers:

1. the Common Cither with four choirs of strings. It is tuned variously, sometimes to b g d' e', and then termed an Italian Cither; and sometimes to a g d' e', then called a French Cither.

This four-choired type is a rather ignoble kind of instrument played by cobblers and gardeners.

2. the cither with five choirs of strings. It is tuned to d b g d' e'; F e c g a; and occasionally also to G f# d a b.

3. the Six-choired Cither. It is tuned in various ways:
   a. the old Italians tuned it to a c' b g d' e'
   b. Sixtus Kargel of Strassburg, to b G d g d' e'.
   c. or it was tuned after the five-choired instrument, to G d b g d' e'. This cither is much easier to play.

4. the Large Six-choired Cither. It is twice as large as the preceding six-choired cither and is tuned a fourth lower, namely to f# D A d a b.

In all, this instrument it almost the length of two forearms. It is to be found on plate V.

5. There is yet a larger kind of cither with twelve choirs of strings. It produces a strong and magnificent sound like a harpsichord. A distinguished court instrumentalist named Domenicus has an instrument of this kind in Prague. It is said to be almost as long as a bass viol da gamba. A drawing of it is to be found on plate VII.

About three years ago an Englishman came to Germany with a very small cither (see plate XVI) the back of which is left half open from bottom to top, without being glued on. He could produce a strange but very lovely and beautiful sound on this instrument, playing with a certain trembling of the hand. This fine vibrato effect might now similarly be practised by many good lutenists.

This instrument is tuned much the same as the four-choired lutes of ancient times, only an octave higher. The treble strings are tuned to g", the seconds to d", thirds to a' and the fourth strings, to f'. The third choir is occasionally raised a semitone to b flat, and as then called "in corda valle". This is very common on lutes in France. And on this cither, brass and steel strings of size no. 11 are used for the treble strings, no. 8 for the seconds, no. 5 for the thirds and no. 10 for the fourth strings (for the fourth choir is tuned only a second lower than the treble strings or first choir).

XXXII
the Harp
(plates XVIII, XIX)

The Harp, or Arpa (from ἁρπάζω, or rapio, since the strings are plucked by the fingers); in Greek, κιθάρα; in French, un harpe; Italian, cetera or arpa; Spanish, harpa; Latin, cithara—as it was also called by the ancients. Thus Hieronymus writes, "Citharam Hebraeorum habuisse 24 chordas vel plures (licet Orpheus septem dundaxat Chordis Cytharam pulsasse dicatur, teste Virgilio, 6 Aeneid:

> Threicius longa cum veste sacerdos
> Obloquitur numeris septem discrimina vocum'.

Ex morticinis animalium intestinis desiccatis, subtiliatis ac tortis, quae fides dicuntur. Hae fides digitorum variis, tinnulisque ictibus in diversis modis tacta pulsantur." See Pliny, chap. 7, 56 Turneb. 19 chap. 30. In a letter to Cardanus, Hieronymus also writes that the cithara was constructed in the form and shape of the Greek letter, Delta, which is not unlike our present harps.

There are now three kinds of harps:

1. the common single harp, which has 24 or several more strings ranging from F to c" or a", and which is without chromatic tones. (plate XVIII).

2. the large Double Harp or harpa doppia (plate XIX), which has a solid body and offers all chromatic tones. (The strings for the chromatic tones lie somewhat closer to the sounding board (18) than the other strings, but along the bridge they all lie evenly.)

On the side for the left hand it has strings on the following tones:

and on the side for the right hand:

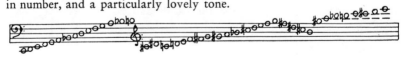

3. The Irish Harp, harpa irlandica, the structure and form of which are shown on plate XVIII, has rather thick brass strings forty-three in number, and a particularly lovely tone.

XXXIII

the Scheitholt

(plate XXI)

Although this instrument really ought to be treated where other such vulgar instruments are described, still I wanted to give some description of it here. It is quite like a board or log and, like a monochord, is set together very simply from three or four thin slabs of wood. At its top it has a small neck into which the pegs are set. It is fitted with three or four brass strings. Three strings are tuned in unison and the middle one can be made to sound a fifth higher by means of a little neck fastened into the fingerboard. If desired, the fourth string can be added tuned an octave higher. The right-hand thumb strums on all these strings together down near the bridge, and a smooth little stick, held in the left hand, is set against the strings, the melody being produced by the contact of the stick with the frets, of brass wire.

XXXIV

the Trumpet Marine

(plate XXI)

The Trumpet Marine, which originated from the monochord, is called the Magas or Magadis by Glareanus (after the terminology of Suida) in book 1 chapter 17 of his "Dodecachordon", to which I refer for the following description: (19).

Today the Germans, French and Netherlanders make use of an instrument which they call the Tympanischiza. It is made out of three thin slabs of wood set together in an extended pyramidal form; is tapered lengthwise; and over the side facing upwards (called the sounding-board) is placed a long gut string. This string is made to sound when stroked by a bow of horsehair rubbed with rosin.

Some persons use another string, half as long, on the instrument so that the first string, together with its octave, will produce an even stronger sound.

In Athenaeus' writings, at the place (20) where he deals with various kinds of instruments, he mentions the Trigonus, included by Plato under the πολύχορδα, or polychorda, in the eighth part of his "De Republica".

But I believe that this last-mentioned instrument is very ancient.

Minstrels play the trumpet marine in the streets, setting its top end, called the neck (into which the pegs are placed) against their chests, and extending its triangular base out forward. They support the instrument in the left hand, pressing easily and lightly on the strings at the various nodal points and sections (21) along its body (and these are referred to as frets on lutes and cithers); and they draw the bow back and forth across the strings with the right hand.

The lower end of the largest string is fastened near the bottom of the instrument and extends up to the end set against the player's chest. The string is pressed on here and there along its length by the thumb of the left hand, and melodies are produced by this means. The bow, drawn over the strings by the right hand, is held very high—between the left hand and the very top of the instrument. The trumpet marine sounds much more pleasant from a distance than when one listens to it close by.

Players are able to play in both the ionian and hypoionian modes very easily on this instrument, just as on trumpets, bagpipes and other such instruments, but can not play the other modes so well.

And though, to be sure, those who are inexperienced in music can only play the thirds, fourths, fifths and octaves of the open strings and are not able to find tones and semitones well, still anyone who applies himself with diligence will be able to play them also (21) even though semitones cannot very clearly be discerned on the instrument because of the buzzing and snarling sound produced by the string.

This buzzing and snarling is caused by a small bent piece of wood set under the string down toward its lower end, much like the bridge of a violin. The thick little tab or foot of this piece of wood is set loosely against the instrument such that the other little tab, which has a surface of ivory or other such hard material, vibrates against the surface of the sounding-board when the string is stroked by the bow; and this causes a shaking and snarling sound.

I had to laugh (says Glareanus further) about the way this instrument was designed. But try as I may, I still have not been able to determine why this rattling sound is not produced on all the nodal points along the string.

Occasionally the players also set a tiny nail into the bottom of the loose tab, so that the shaking and snarling against the body can be heard all the more strongly.

And this is just as on the harp, for the strings of the harp also rattle and crackle if they come into contact with the pegs with which they are fastened into the frame of the instrument, at the bottom. This rattling is usually referred to as "harfenierend" or a harp-like sound.

The length of this three-edged monochord is almost five feet, and its three slabs of wood are each five inches wide at the base and two inches wide at the top. And so much from Glareanus.

The trumpet marine, as I have seen it (and I am in possession of one) is seven feet, three inches long. At its triangular base, each edge is seven inches wide, but hardly two inches wide at the top. It is spanned with four strings, such that the principal and longest string is tuned to C, the second to c, the third to g and the fourth to c'. The upper three strings are used as drones, always sounding c g c'; but the actual melody is produced on the lowest string by contact of the thumb. And when this instrument is heard from a distance it sounds no other than as if four trumpets were blowing together in lovely concord. Otherwise in all respects it is the same as was indicated above by Glareanus, in German translation.

XXXV

the Monochord

(plate XXXIX)

The Monochord is described by the above mentioned Sebastian Virdung as a quadrangular frame, like a box or chest, over which is stretched a string. Through proportions, this string establishes and verifies all consonances. It is divided off into proportional sections by a compass, and a fret is made to mark each point thus arrived at. Each fret is placed at the correct point below the string and produces its pitch exactly as given by the measure of Nature. Since more will be said about this at another place and also because it is dealt with by various other writers, I regard it unnecessary to treat it in greater detail here.

XXXVI

the Clavichord

(plate XV)

The Clavichord was based on the monochord and its keys arranged in accordance with it (and set to the scale of Guido, which had only twenty tones). The clavichord has keys in place of the frets of the monochord. Only twenty keys, in the diatonic genus, were made for it originally. Of these, just the b-flat and b'-flat were fitted with black keys: for there were no more than three kinds of semitones in the octave — a-b flat, b-c, and e-f — as on very old organs. But subsequently the matter was further thought over, and, based on Boethius, semitones of the chromatic genus were added such that its keyboard then contained the following keys:

It will be unknown to few that today all clavichords start with C at the bottom and go up to a'', c''' or d''', and even to f'''.

Just as a good mastery of the lute is the basis from which one learns all other similar stringed instruments—such as the pandora, theorbo, penorcon, Mandürchen, cither, harp, and also violins and viols; and similarly, just as one who has mastered the flute is then able to make rapid progress with all other instruments with finger-holes—like the cornet, shawm, bumbarde, bassoon, dulcian, rackett and the like; thus also the clavichord is the basic instrument of all the keyboard instruments, including the organ, harpsichord, spinet, virginals, etc. Beginning organ students are first taught the clavichord. This is chiefly because the clavichord has no quills—and these usually cause much trouble and displeasure to the player; and it is also because its strings remain more constant than those of the harpsichord and spinet, which require many and frequent tunings. Clavichords often need not be tuned for long periods of time, and this is particularly advantageous for beginning students who are not yet able to tune and quill instruments.

In plate XV, no. 2, is shown a clavichord which some thirty years ago was brought from Italy to Meissen. On this instrument the choirs of strings for the d's and a's of all octaves are struck by just a single key. This is in order to avoid the κακοφωνίαν and unpleasant sound caused when two keys strike a choir at once in places in the music where seconds above these tones must be sounded at the same time (as, for example, in syncopations (22) and cadences).

Except for this, however, multiple keys are retained on this clavichord, with two, three or even four for each choir of strings; but these need not all be used in dissonances.

This year I had a clavichord (in size and form like no. 2 of plate XV) built by a good instrument maker, and on it there were separate keys not only for d# and e-flat, g# and a-flat, and b-flat and a# but also for c# and d-flat, f# and g-flat, and with a special key for e# and b#, all just as on the Clavicembalum Universale, to be dealt with in chapter XL.

XXXVII

the Symphony

(plate XIV)

The Symphony is generally, though incorrectly, designated by the term, Instrument (as is the case with the harpsichord, virginals and spinet). This term is a quite general one and is applied to all musical instruments, as was mentioned in the beginning of this book. Therefore it can not be made to refer just to instruments like the symphony and harpsichord.

———

XXXVIII

the Spinet

(plate XIV)

The Spinet (Italian, spinetto) is a small quadrangular instrument which is tuned an octave or a fifth higher than the ordinary pitch. It is generally placed on top of larger keyboard instruments. In Italy, however, the large as well as the small quadrangular instruments are named spinets without distinction.

In England all such instruments, be they small or large, are termed Virginals.

In France, Espinettes.

In the Netherlands, Clavicymbels and also Virginals.

In Germany they are called Instruments, like all other keyboard instruments.

XXXIX

the Harpsichord

(plate VI)

The Harpsichord—also Clavicembalum or Gravicembalum—is a longish instrument and is called by some a "Flügel", since it is in the shape of a wing; and by others a "Schweinskopf" (but this is poor usage) because it is pointed and tapered at one end like the head of a boar. It has a strong, bright sound, lovelier than the others because of its double, triple and even quadruple strings. I once saw a harpsichord each key of which had two gut strings in unison and one at the fifth and octave; and this sounded very lovely and fine.

XL

the Clavicembalum Universale or Perfectum

The harpsichord, symphony and the like, otherwise called Instruments (though incorrectly, as mentioned before) are rather incomplete and imperfect in that they do not afford chromatic tones such as can be produced on lutes and viols da gamba. On this account various harpsichords, in accordance with the specifications of good organists, have been provided with two different keys for the d#, such that in the aeolian mode transposed a fourth lower, the third falling between the b and f'# may be had in a pure and correct form.

In my modest opinion, it would be very advisable to make double keys for the d# and also the g# on the positive and organ as well as on the harpsichord. (This is even more necessary for the organ than for the harpsichord, the strings of which can easily be retuned and adjusted.) Thus in the hypodorian mode transposed a second lower to f, one would be able to obtain the minor third above the f quite justly and purely from the a-flat key which would be made next to the g#; and one might well have many more variations of this kind in the chromatic genus.

In Prague I have seen a harpsichord with choirs of strings tuned in unison, at Carl Luyton's, distinguished composer and organist of His Imperial Roman Majesty. This instrument was very finely and skillfully wrought thirty years ago in Vienna. Not only did it have all chromatic tones, such as b-flat, c#, d#, f# and g# in double form throughout, but it was also provided with a special chromatic tone necessary for the enharmonic genus, between the e's and f's, such that the instrument had 77 keys in all in its four octaves.

Since this instrument is seldom encountered, I wished to designate these keys here: (23)

C^s	D^s	E_2	F^s	G^s	B_2	H_2	c^s	d^s	e_2	f_2	g^s	b^2	h_2	$c^{s'}$
C_2	D_2		E_2	G_2	B		c_2	d_2		f_2	g_2	b		$c_2{'}$
C	D	E	F	G	A	H c		d	e	f	g	a	h c	

and so on up to c'''.

But because in this diagram the various chromatic tones and the keys for them are designated in terms of their relation with the basic tones and their keys, I modestly wished to show their actual order in the next diagram, for the benefit of those who desire to think this over further:

3	5	8	11	14	16	19
d^b	d#	e#	g^b	a^b	a#	b#

2	6		10	13	17	
c#	e^b		f#	g#	b^b	

1	4	7	9	12	15	18	20
c	d	e	f	g	a	b	c

etc.

And so that everyone will be able to orient himself better in this (for the excellent and skilled composer, Luca Marenzio, has written some very beautiful chromatic madrigals) I have put it down in notation here:

This harpsichord can be raised seven times in pitch—namely from c through c♯, d♭, d, e♭ and d♯ up to e—thus amounting to three whole tones. This can occur with almost no other instrument. In this form all three genera of modulation—the diatonic, chromatic and enharmonic—can be brought to play. This instrument might justly be called an Instrumentum Perfectum—if not perfectissimum—because such variation through all accidentals and chromatic tones is not to be had on other instruments.

(24)

Gambas and especially lutes, of course, afford all chromatic tones; yet their tuning is not as pure and true as that of a harpsichord of this kind. This is because the frets on gambas and lutes are all equally spaced (though the nearer the bridge, the closer the spacing—and this goes without saying). Therefore the chromatic tones produced from them are neither semitonia majora nor minora—neither large nor small half-tones—but should be termed intermedia, or intermediate; for each of the frets is spaced at the interval of 4¹/₂ commata, while the semitonium majus is properly 5, and the semitonium minore, 4 commata in size.

But then the frets are false only by a half-comma on either side, and this does not disturb the ear very much, since the discrepancy can not be discerned very clearly.

Thus the large semitone sounds just as well as the small one produced on the same fret—just as though it were correctly tuned. The main reason for this is that the player can influence the pitch of the strings by the position of his fingers on the frets. This cannot be done on the harpsichord and organ, for the strings and pipes of these instruments cannot be adjusted in pitch during the course of playing, but on the contrary must remain set as they are tuned.

The chromatic genus thus cannot entirely be adhered to on keyboard instruments unless they have differentiated keys for chromatic tones. If it is desired to play chromatically on the lute, all its frets would have to be taken off and it would have to be played without them entirely.

And Christopher Cornet, a distinguished musician at Kassel, told me that in Italy he saw a similar instrument (or spinet, as it is called there) belonging to an Italian named Julius Caesar.

He also told me that of all the nationalities in the world, the Greeks sing the most beautifully and perfectly together with these instruments, for there were four Greek musicians serving at Kassel at that time.

Some few years ago a magnificent positive was brought from Italy to the court of the archduke at Graz. On this instrument all chromatic tones are similarly to be found double and complete; and it is said to be a superb piece of craftsmanship.

———

XLI

the Clavicytherium

The Clavicytherium is tapered at the end like a harpsichord, only its body, containing the sounding-board and strings, is constructed upright—as may be seen from plate XV. It produces a sound almost the same as that of cithers and harps.

XLII

the Claviorganum

The Claviorganum is a harpsichord or symphony provided with various ranks of pipes, as in a positive, and these are built in along with the strings. It looks the same as a harpsichord or symphony. It has bellows which are attached to the back of its body or else set inside.

XLIII

the Arpichordum

The Arpichordum is a symphony or virginal on which a harp-like sound is produced by means of a special stop which governs metal jacks under the strings.

XLIV

the Geigenwerk, Geigeninstrument,
Geigenclavicymbel; or Violin-Clavier
(plate III)

This Violin-Clavier looks entirely the same in shape and proportions as the ordinary harpsichord and is the same in size, such that it can be set on tables and carried easily from place to place. A single person is able to play on it what otherwise would require five of six violins. This instrument was first devised and constructed by a burger of Nuremberg, Hans Hayden by name. The idea for it came, perhaps, from the construction of the common lyra (4), the strings of which are made to sound by contact with a wheel. Some writers, such as Galileo, believe that violin-claviers like this have been contrived even before our time. But be that as it may, my opinion in the matter is that even if similar instruments did exist before, they can not have been as excellent as this one, which the named Hans Hayden has really succeeded in making work.

In place of jacks, this violin-clavier has five or six steel wheels smoothly covered with parchment rubbed with rosin (just as is the violin bow). These wheels are governed by another large wheel and various rollers lying under the sounding-board, and are pedaled below by the player himself, or else pumped up above by a bellows-pumper, in such a fashion that the wheels remain in constant motion.

Now when a key is depressed, the corresponding string comes into contact with one of the revolving wheels, producing a sound as if a bow had been drawn over the string.

The low strings are of thick brass and steel wound in pure parchment. Thus the lowest strings are almost as thick as the heavy strings of the bass viol, some of them going down as low as F and D; but further up they gradually diminish in thickness, such that above in the discant range, only plain strong steel strings without parchment are to be found.

In order that those who have not yet seen such an instrument may learn of the advantages it has over other keyboard instruments with respect to dynamic moderation of tones, I wish to set down here the very words and thoughts of its distinguished inventor, which were printed in the year 1610 in a little booklet; and thus submit the matter to the judgement of the reader.

"In recent times especially, composers have been devoting most of their efforts to choral music and have brought it to such a height of perfection that there is no longer much further to be done. But great deficiencies are still found in instruments. For instance, instruments are failing in the most beautiful of expressive effects—the dynamic moderation of tones; and up to now, of all the skilled players of keyboard instruments, not one has attempted to remedy this shortcoming in making such dynamic change possible on these instruments.

"How important it is to give form and shape to musical lines will be known by those who train vocalists and boy singers in chapels. Now almost everyone knows how unsatisfactory it is when an orator talks on and on in the same tone, rather than pronouncing with a rising or falling inflection, in accordance with the requirements of the text and of the Affections; and if this is annoying to hear in speaking, it is even more the case with singing.

"All keyboard instruments—even the organ, most dignified of instruments—have the disadvantage that their tones cannot be moderated dynamically and cannot be made loud or soft in sound: for a pipe produces and holds its sound in a constant volume, and just as long as the player keeps its key down. It is thus impossible to strengthen or soften this sound. But on the violin the sound can be regulated by heavy or light bowing. The player of keyboard instruments is then restricted in that he cannot give expression to his Affections, showing whether sad, joyous, serious or playful thoughts are in him; while this can all be indicated quite clearly on violins (even though texts can not be rendered on them). Such expression can only be effected by means of actual dynamic moderation. And though by changing the registration on the organ one is able to obtain now a still, soft and lovely sound, and now great noise and clamor, indeed this does not amount to dynamic moderation: for the organ remains soft or loud within a given strength of volume, producing an unmoderated and constant volume of sound—just as was said above on varied speech.

"Nor can the strings of keyboard instruments be made to sound softer or louder than the usual volume produced by their keys. And then, too, the sound cannot be sustained, for as soon as the strings are struck, it diminishes and disappears such that no long note-values can be continued evenly in volume on these instruments.

"This decreasing and fading of sound is contrary to proper dynamic moderation; for one should be able to increase the tone from soft to loud.

"Thus when it is desirable to maintain a tone completely for a whole beat, it is necessary that this tone be divided up and struck repeatedly. But this is contrary to the nature of the stately and grave music of motets and other such music—though it can be made use of quite well in passamezzi, gaillards and other dances.

"Now on this violin-clavier, sound can both be continued indefinitely and moderated dynamically. This can be done not alone for the duration of a breve, but even for a longa and maxima tied together—and not even on violins is this possible, because of the shortness of the bow.

"And even though the words of the text cannot be produced on this violin-clavier, still, by playing roughly or gently on the keys the player is able to give expression to his feelings, and show whether sad or happy thoughts are in him. So much for the first point.

"Second, the player is able to alter the tempo at his own pleasure, making it now slow and now again faster. This too is helpful in moving the Affections, and it can also be done on similar instruments.

"Third, a voice can suddenly be made to sound loud, then soft, and then loud again when the text requires.

"Fourth, the instrument is very amusing, and is astonishing to hear; for even though it has only one manual and a single set of strings, one person alone can make it sound none other than as if two different sets of strings were sounding, or even two different players were playing antiphonally.

"Fifth, one can also produce an echo on it just as if it were an echo from the woods or valleys.

"Sixth, one can make it sound like other instruments, especially like the lute.

"Seventh, one is very well able to lead a chorale tune in one part on the instrument—be it the bass, tenor, or discant—such that it is heard more strongly than the other parts.

"Eighth, the vibrato effect produced on the organ by the tremulant can be produced on this instrument just by using one hand and without recourse to special registration.

"Ninth and Tenth, it can be made well to sound like a peasant lyra (4); and tenth, like a bagpipe and shawm, such that it can be used to please women and children who otherwise do not greatly care for music—and also for the amusement of very respectable people when they are a little tipsy from a good drink.

"Eleventh, it can sound like a cither, just as when young fellows go serenading.

"Twelfth, it is also good for imitating the viola bastarda.

"Thirteenth, one can play court music and band music on it, making it sound as if twelve trumpets and clarinos were playing together. Then one can use small kettle drums with this violin-clavier—and some of them are provided with such drums, which are activated by a stop; and this does not sound badly at all.

"Fourteenth, it has only a single string to each key. When covered it produces a soft, still sound like violins and is lovely to hear in a small chamber; but if desired it may be used opened and made to sound so loud that it can be heard very well in an entire ensemble of singers and instruments.

"The player can do all this and still more on this instrument, although it has only an ordinary manual and requires no special finger technique. But one must play on the manual lightly and not with full weight. It is necessary that the player devote diligent practise to the coordination of his fingers and feet, and he must accustom himself to the two wooden pedals governing the wheels until he is able to tread them constantly and in accordance with the tempo, whether set by himself or by the other musicians of the ensemble. In this way he will be able better to remain in tempo. He must pay good attention not to strike the keys too hard or soft with the fingers, lest some of the strings rattle too loud and the others respond too little or not at all. This cannot be done by everyone at first without diligent and steady practising.

"But when one becomes better accustomed to this instrument and understands the dynamic moderation which is to be had on it, one has need of no other instrument. It is also all the more agreeable in that it does not require as much tuning as lutes, violins and stringed keyboard instruments; for its strings are not of gut, but of metal and steel—and these improve with wear and do not soon get out of tune.

"And although this instrument may have been falsely judged by some persons before they became accustomed to it, or by others who either are vexed with practising or are not able to make progress with it at all, I pray they will not bring it into ill repute and entreat them to have patience until they have accustomed themselves to it and have learned how to play it correctly. Then I know they will make use of it with interest and pleasure and do not doubt that they will be thankful to me for having made dynamic moderation possible on a keyboard instrument. And to state the matter frankly, I have indeed encountered persons who at first thought nothing at all of this instrument—not just while it was too difficult for them, but because out of sheer laziness and neglect they did not want to exert any effort on it; but after they took it in hand and practised it diligently, they became so fond of it that they could not have their fill of playing it, and even came to prefer it much to a good clavichord or harpsichord."

XLV
the Regal
(plate IV)

The term, regal, may apply to the reed stops generally found forward in the breast-works of the organ. But this term is also used in royal chapels to designate an instrument in the shape of a small and longish chest containing one or more ranks of reeds, and with two sets of bellows attached in back. This instrument can be set on a table and is very convenient for use in ensembles—more so than a harpsichord, which is much too soft in full ensembles and the strings of which cannot well prolong their sound more than half a measure.

On the regal, however, the sound continues as long as the key is depressed (as on the organ); and this is particularly necessary in ensembles. The regal can be made very soft by placing its cover on, and by taking it off it can be made loud enough to sound clearly in a full and well-appointed ensemble of singers and players. It is heard with great pleasure before court banquets and at affairs of honor, and may be used almost better than a positive in churches both large and small.

I believe it would be better to name this instrument a regal-works and to call the organ regal stops by the term, regal-pipes, in order better to distinguish the one from the other.

There are regals with only one rank of small reeds in 8-foot tuning; with two ranks, the one in 8-foot, the other in 4-foot tuning; and with three ranks, making a range of three octaves, of which the lowest is in 16-foot tuning. In some there is a fourth register consisting of small repeating stops, and this sounds very much like an organ in very soft registration.

The structure of the frame of the regal and its stops is quite diverse, and it would be too discursive to specify all the varieties of these here.

Of these instruments, however, those built up to now in Vienna, Austria, are rather superior to the others; but nevertheless, many magnificent regals made by other masters may be found and can be played with delight—especially when the lowest regal pipe, the 8-foot C, is made of tin, measures about 5 or 5^1/$_2$ inches in length, is squared and completely closed at the top, and is perforated with three, four or five small holes, as on the dulcian or bassoon—and more of this will be shown in the Fourth Part. The sound of this is indeed very lovely.

These pipes may also be found somewhat shorter and entirely open on top, and are sometimes wrought out of brass in different ways; but these are not as lovely in sound as the covered reeds.

At a famous town not far from here, a certain person two years ago started to build very fine regals with wooden pipes. These are very lovely in tone, and can easily be transported from one place to another.

The very small regals built directly on to the bellows were first invented in Nuremberg and Augsburg, and are, to be sure, very convenient to carry and handy to move; but the reeds on them are made very small—hardly an inch high—in order to fit into the chamber of the instrument; and they are almost too jarring in sound.

In Regensburg, Bavaria, I have seen a regal which was planned and constructed by a monk. On the stops, the mouthpieces were of wood and the reeds were of the same cane used for the reeds of wind instruments such as dulcians, krummhorns, shawms and bagpipes, etc. Its regal pipes did not stand separate, but were bored right in through the body of the regal such that the sound issued out of the bottom of the instrument. It had a lovely manner and a very soft tone, but because of the cane, the reeds were very changeable and had always to be retuned.

And here I must not forget to mention that some believe the regal to have its name from the fact that the first instrument of its kind was offered by its inventor as a special present to his king. Thus it was named "Regale", that is to say, dignum rege, or worthy of a king.

There is now a distinguished organ and instrument maker at a certain electoral court who has made known his intention of constructing a regal which will not get out of tune for long periods of time, regardless whether it is brought from the cold into the warmth or vice-versa. If this could really be done, it would be worth its weight in gold; but I surely doubt it, for I know only too well how much difficulty is caused the organist or director of an ensemble when several regals are to be played together in churches or at court dinners—and especially when in winter a regal must be brought out of the coldness of the church into a warm dining room. It is indeed true that metal pipes are forced down in pitch to such an extent by the cold of winter that they sink by half a semitone, if not more. (This is particularly true of small churches, into which the cold of winter and the heat of summer penetrate easily; but less so of large vaulted churches, which tend to be nice and cool in summer, like cellars, and do not become extremely cold in winter.) This changing in pitch can be observed on wind instruments such as cornets, flutes, trombones, bumbardes and bassoons, and especially on positives, even though these are kept in warm chambers; and when the stoves are going, these instruments become even sharper from the great warmth. And it is really remarkable that all the pipes of the organ, often amounting to several hundred or even thousand (with 3742 pipes being found on the Danzig organ) sharpen in the summer and flatten in the winter, all deviating similarly from the pitch to which they were tuned.

On the other hand, all reeds, of the regal as well as of the organ, flatten in the heat of summer and sharpen in the cold of winter. The cause for this will be discussed to some extent in the Fourth Part following. Causam sive limus inquirere, inquit Dominus S.C. eam in discrimine metalli consistere arbitror, quod stannum vel plumbum calore contrahatur, aes Lypsium vero dilatetur. Id quod disci posset ex artificibus qui ista metalla tractant. Causa in aerem conferri per se non potest, nisi quando propter calorem et frigus metalla afficit, alias si aer calore dilataretur, in plumbo et aere cyprio eundem effectum produceret. Sed hoc non fit. Ergo tantum in metallis causa quaerenda.

But since many different points of view are held on this matter, I regard it as entirely unnecessary to discuss it at greater length here.

It may be demonstrated further that the above is actually true: for when a metal pipe is touched by an organ maker while he is tuning or otherwise, it directly changes in pitch due to the warmth of his hand, becoming a little sharp; and then after it is left alone for a little, it returns to its normal pitch. This may also be clearly observed on wind instruments such as the flute and cornet in particular. And though some believe that organs and positives containing nothing but wooden pipes are not subject to such great variability, still experience shows that in organs in which various separate wooden pipes are found together with the metal pipes, both kinds deviate similarly in pitch according to the weather.

And since up to now no one has been able to establish the true cause for such variation and change, this must be taken for one of the extraordinary works of God.

And all this was so strange that I was reluctant to believe it until I actually saw it myself.

XLVI
of Various Other, especially Ancient, Instruments

In plates XXXII, XXXIII and XXXIV of the Theatre of Instruments I have also included several drawings of ancient instruments found in an old book written in German by Sebastian Virdung, a priest at Amberg, and printed at Basel in the year 1511. And since I could find no other information as to how these obsolete instruments were used, I have included here word for word the description of them found in this book. (25)

the Chorus

no. 1

The Chorus was an instrument with two tubes joined by a mouth-piece at one end and by a large bell from which the sound came, at the other.

———————

the Psalterium

no. 2

and Psalterium Decachordum

nos. 3 & 4

The Psalterium was formed in two ways—triangular, like the Triangle (nos. 2 and 3); and square (no. 4), as is to be seen from the drawing.

In the above mentioned book, the author writes the following:

I have never seen the psalterium now in use in any but a triangular form. I am of the opinion that the Virginal, which is operated by keys and has strings which are struck by feather quills, originated from the psalterium. Although the virginal resembles the clavichord in that it is built in a long case, other of its characteristics relate it more closely to the psalterium. Among these characteristics are that it has a separate string for each tone, and that each of its strings is successively longer than the preceding, with the result that its frame is also almost triangular in shape.

the Cithara Hieronymi
(nos. 5, 6, 7, 8)

I find old harps formed in four ways; and although these harps may not be entirely similar in shape to our modern instruments (and this could also be the fault of the artist's drawing) still they too tended toward the triangular form. And even though modern harps have more strings, the old harps were much better in sound, more artful in construction, and were easier to learn to play.

---

the Tympanum Hieronymi
(no. 9)

In this book we find drawn the Tympanum (very frequently used in praise of God the Almighty, and often mentioned in the Scriptures) as a long pipe with at one end a mouthpiece into which one blows, and at the other, two holes from which the sound and wind issue. The tympanum was constructed such that a woman could carry it in one hand.

But in our own times, the term, tympanum, refers to large kettle-drums made of copper caldrons and covered with a stretched piece of calfhide on which one beats with drum sticks. Kettle-drums are used together with wind instruments at the courts of princes and great lords for processionals, banquets and dances, and are also used in war. They are great rattletraps. Then there are other drums as well, called snare drums, and together with which, dwarfpipes or Swiss pipes were used.

There is yet another kind of drum, a tiny drum frequently used by the French and Lowlanders (plate IX). A Schwegel or stamentien-pipe is used with it. The drum and pipe are both held by the left hand. Three fingers of this hand hold the pipe by its three holes, one of them being in back; and all kinds of dances and songs can be played on the instrument. The drum stick is beaten on the drumhead by the right hand at the same time.

the Tuba Hieronymi
(no. 10)

Hieronymus says that the tuba had three mouthpieces, signifying the Father, Son and Holy Ghost in Trinity; and the four ends from which the sound escaped were supposed to symbolize the four Evangelists.

---

the Organum Hieronymi
(no. 11)

the Fistula Hieronymi
(no. 12)

He describes the fistula as an instrument in the shape of a carpenter's square, which is to signify the Holy Cross. The quadrangular instrument with twelve pipes is supposed to stand for Christ and the Twelve Apostles.

---

the Cimbalum Hieronymi
(no. 13)

The twelve pipes of the cimbalum, like those of the organum, are to symbolize the Twelve Apostles. Number fourteen is a form of the old violin.

To what purpose and in what fashion all these instruments were used, I do not know; and I have neither heard nor seen any of them. The poets have described still many more instruments with singular names, and I have no way of knowing anything about them further than that they were used as musical instruments. And whether they were better or worse, more beautiful or ugly, more subtle or coarse in form than our instruments, I have also been unable to learn up to the present, from any author who has written anything about this.

But I believe that in the next hundred years, musical instruments will be just as artfully and beautifully made as any of those which Orpheus, Linus, Pan, Apollo and all the Poets could have seen or heard, and what is more, that they will be better than they could even have regarded as possible.

One encounters many foolish devices which are also regarded as musical instruments—like the Acherhorn, sleighbells, triangles, hunting horns (plate XXII), field horns, cowbells, noise-makers (plate XXXIII), little quill pipes, bird-callers, the bird-fowlers' lark-pipes, the hollow bones of titmice and quail, and pipes made from blades of straw or the leaves and green bark of trees.

And up to here, the words of
Sebastian Virdung.

It is unnecessary to write anything about the various other kinds of instruments found in the Theatre of Instruments (the dulcimer, plate XVIII; the peasants lyra (4), key-fiddle (26), strawfiddle (6), little cymbals and bells, musical balls, and Basque tambourine, plate XXII; army or kettle drums, snare drums, and the anvil, plate XXIII; and also other Muscovite, Turkish, strange and foreign instruments, plates XXIX, XXX and XXXI). Some of these justly could be called vulgar and crude instruments, or as Sebastian Virdung calls them, ridiculous instruments, since they are known to all and do not actually have anything to do with music. The anvil was included in the Theatre because Pythagoras, from examining the difference in sound produced by its hammers, was enabled to discover the basis for the difference in musical consonances (the octave, fifth and fourth), and what the proportions of these differences were. More about this may be found in Boethius, book I, chapters 10 and 11 of his "De Musica", and in Seth Calvisius' "Exercitatio".

XLVII

on Organs

(plates II, XXIV — XXVIII) (27)

In Book One, part one, to be sure, the writings of various authors have been referred to with regard to the organ; and since it is essential that this instrument be treated more closely than could be done in the second part of this volume, it will be dealt with in the third and fourth parts following.

A drawing of the positive may be found on plate IV.

XLVIII

About the Positive with a Single Rank of Pipes
and Three Different Registers (plate XXXVII)

I want to mention here that an old positive with fine, artful workmanship has come into my hands. It is said to have been built by a monk, and was presented to King Christian IV of Denmark. (Its form and structure may be seen from plate I.)

This positive has only one rank of pipes—namely, the open 2-foot diapason; and though it has but 38 keys, from F to a", there is another higher octave of pipes placed over the top center of the chest and set around in a spiral arrangement.

Each single pipe has three register couplings, the first giving the correct low fundamental; the second the fifth; and the third the octave above. Each register may be coupled in separately; or then two can be used together; and then all three, such that with one pipe and one key, three distinct pitches can be heard, namely the fundamental, fifth and octave. I leave it up to the clever organist to understand how this functions. I do hope that some instrument maker will undertake to copy this instrument.

Besides that there is another ingenious device on this instrument: when half of the lead weights, each of which is made in two parts, are taken off the bellows, a very soft and quiet tone is produced, sounding none other than as if a set of flutes were playing together.

Technical Remarks
on the Translation

In Parts I and II, the translation was made to follow the layout of the original German as closely as possible, in order to make it easier for the reader to check with the original if desired. In the introduction, however, the paging was not followed.

The English names for the instruments treated are of the translator's choice and for the most part do not occur in the original text.

Where ranges of instruments are specified, the usual symbols are used to indicate the various octaves: capital letters for the great octave; small letters for the small octave; small letters with one dash for the one-line octave, with two dashes for the two-lined octave, etc. These symbols are found in the original essentially the same as they are used today.

Where bracketed numbers appear in the text, they refer to the following editorial notes:

1. Heinrich Pipegrob
2. a chronogram:
   "DIe fVrCht Des Herren Ist Der VVeIsheIt anfang."
3. It is obvious from Praetorius' repeated references to this, that the term, "instrument" referred to key-board instruments in the German of his time and locality. Similarly, "Instrumentist" generally referred to players of these instruments. Thus this does not apply very well in translation. See p. 11 of the text.
4. like a hurdy-gurdy.
5. a keyboard instrument in general.
6. like a xylophone
7. like a hurdy-gurdy
8. Praetorius' error. Shown only on plate VI.
9. falsetto tones: those tones produced outside the natural range of instruments either by overblowing, in the case of high tones, or by the sounding of pedal tones, in the case of the low tones.
10. due to the different arrangement of its holes.

11. A misprint in the original. Praetorius intends to refer to chapter 45.

12. bicinia—two-part pieces
    tricinia—three-part pieces

13. For the most part, the nomenclature of strings and parts of the lute are used as found in Thos. Mace's "Musick's Monument", London. Mace's nomenclature for certain of the parts of the lute is indicated as follows.

> Theorbenkragen—upper head
> body—belly

The term, choir of strings, was for the sake of convenience appropriated from the German "Chorsaite", since no English equivalent was found to exist.

14. In German lute tablature, small letters indicated the position of the fingers on the fretting of the fingerboard:

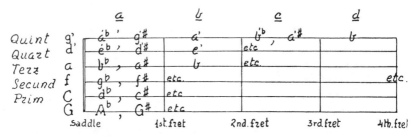

15. e''' undoubtedly intended.

16. The visually difficult charts of ranges appearing in the original are transcribed into a more modern form.

In some cases, only the lowest notes of instruments are indicated in the original, and thus also in the translation.

17. Judging from the diagram of its tuning as given in the Universal Table, open strings must have been used predominantly.

18. The frame was backed by a metal soundingboard.

19. Some of the information following was taken from Glareanus by Praetorius, but not in direct translation, as might be supposed.

20. books IV and XIV, according to Glareanus.

21. This refers to the harmonics produced on the open strings,

> the touched octave equalling the octave of the open string,

the touched fifth equalling the 8ve and 5th of the open string,
the touched fourth equalling the double 8ve of the open string,
etc.

22. suspensions

23. The first diagram is just as in the original, with the b equalling
b-flat, and the h, b-natural.

24. This actually means that 19-tone equal temperament was used
on this instrument, and that all kinds of transposition were possible
on it, each tone being usable as a tonic.

25. What follows is mostly in direct quotation of "Musica Getutscht",
but in Praetorius' more up-to-date German.

26. like a nickel-harp

27. There are numerous errors in Praetorius' references to plate
numberings. Most of these have been corrected in the text of
this translation without comment.

————————

Theater of Instruments or Sciagraphia of Michael Praetorius, consisting of exact drawings and facsimiles of almost all musical instruments presently in use and available in France, England, Germany and other places; also various ancient instruments and instruments from the Indies, all accurately and faithfully drawn to scale and categorized.

Wolfenbüttel, in the year 1620.

This is the correct length and measure in units of half a shoe or half a foot, after the standard of one-quarter of a Braunschweig ell. All the drawings of the following instruments are made in accordance with this measure, which accompanies each drawing in scale.

Old Positive with uniform pipes and three different registers, such that it gives three distinct voicings, on two-foot, one-and-a-half, and one-foot pitch.

Rückpositif of Organ.

Nuremberg Geigenwerk [Piano-Violin].

1. Positive.　　2. Regal.

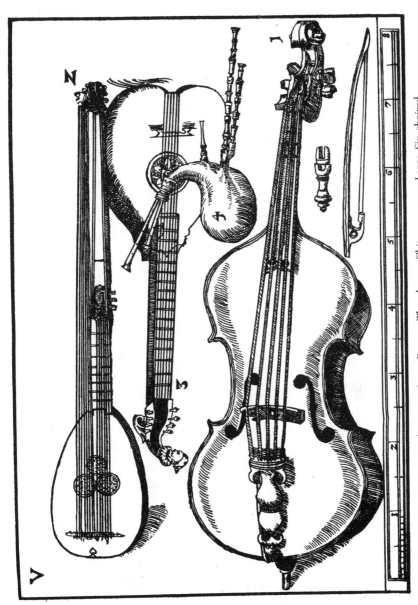

1. Large Contrabass. 2. Long Roman Theorbo or Chitarrone. 3. Large Six-choired Cither. 4. Magdeburg Bagpipe.

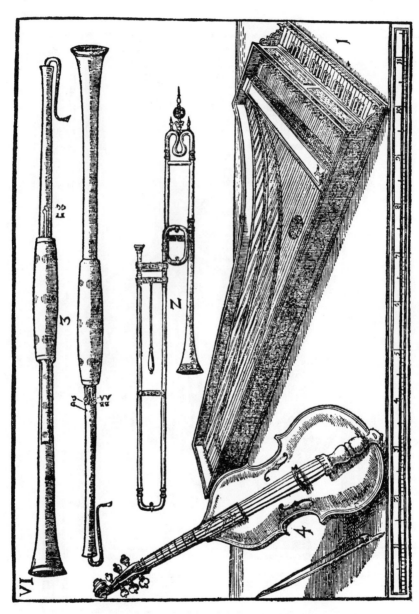

1. Clavicembalo, tuned a fourth below Choral Pitch   2. Octave—Trombone   3. Large
Double Quint—Pommer   4. Violone, large Bass Viol da Gamba.

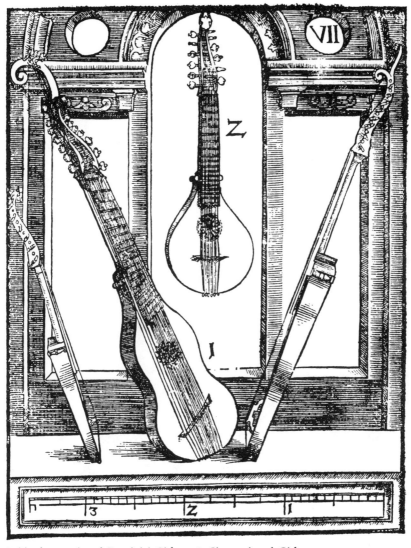

1. Twelve—stringed Dominici Cither   2. Six—stringed Cither.

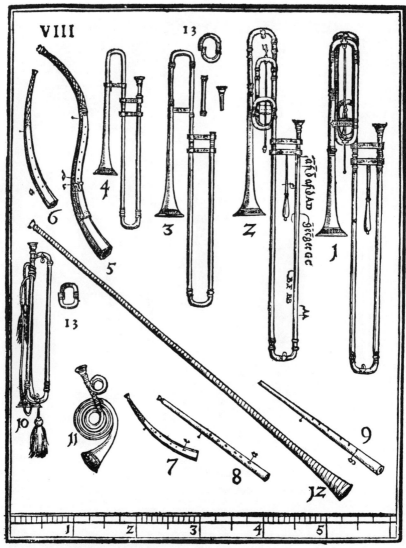

1./2. Quart—Trombones 3. Ordinary Trombones 4. Alto Trombone 5. Large Tenor Cornet 6. Common Cornet 7. Small Discant Cornet, a fifth higher 8. Straight Cornet with Mouthpiece 9. Soft Cornet 10. Trumpet 11. Hunting Trumpet 12. Wooden Trumpet 13. Whole-tone Crook.

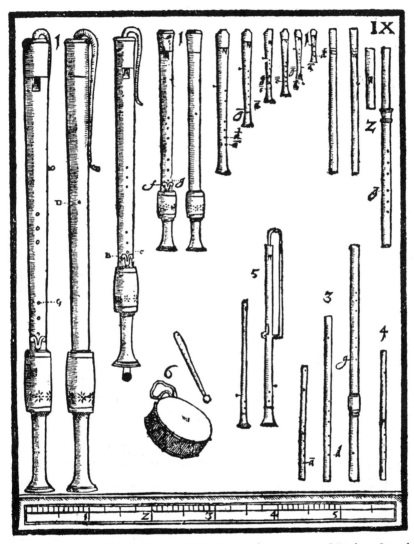

1. Complete Set of Recorders   2. Dulceflutes, the same   3. Complete Set of Transverse Flutes   4. Swiss Pipe   5. Stamentien-pipe, Bass and Discant   6. Small Drum, used with Stamentien-pipes.

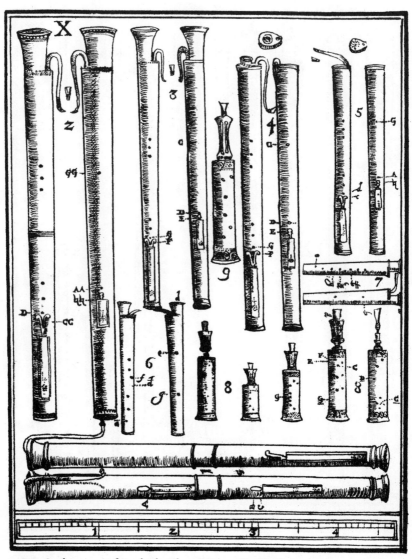

1. Bass Sordune, seen from both sides, GG.   2. Double Bassoon, down to GG.   3. Open Chorist Bassoon, C.   4. Closed Chorist Bassoon, C.   5. Single Kortholt. Tenor to the Chorist Basson, G.   6. Alto, d.   7. Discant or Soprano to the Chorist Basson, a.   8. Set of Racketts.   9. Large Rackett, as low as the very large Bass Bumbarde, CC, in 16-foot pitch.

Note regarding numbers 1 through 5: the letters designate keys which close the holes. In numbers 6 through 8, however, the letters designate holes which remain open.

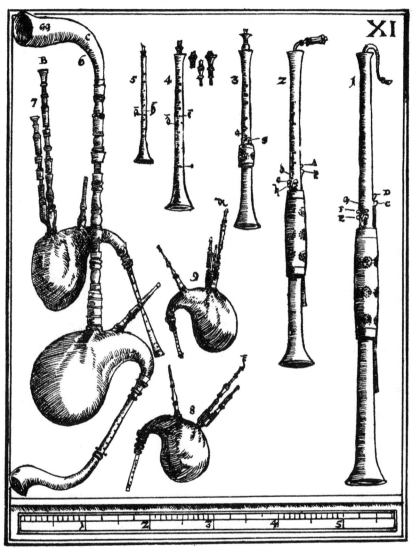

1. Bass Pommer.   2. Basset or Tenor Pommer.   3. Alto Pommer.   4. Discant
Shawm.   5. Small Shawm.   6. Large Bock.   7. Shepherd's Pipe.   8. Hümmelchen (or
small bagpipe).   9. Dudey (or small bagpipe).

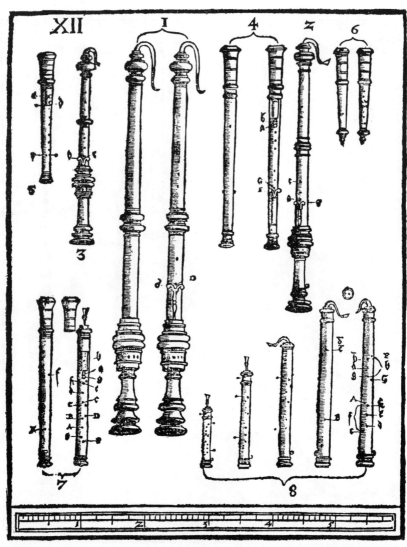

1. Bass Bassanello   2. Tenor and Alto Bassanello   3. Discant Bassanello   4. Bass
Schryari   5. Tenor, Alto Schryari   6. Discant Schryari   7. Kortholt, or Short Pipe
8. Complete Set of Sordunes.

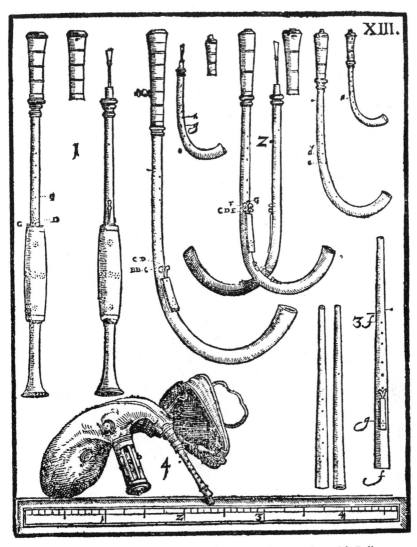

XIII.

1. Nicolo Bassett   2. Krummhorns   3. Soft Cornets   4. Bagpipe with Bellows.

1./2. Spinets or Virginals (commonly called "Instruments") in the correct choir tone. 3. Little Octave Virginal.

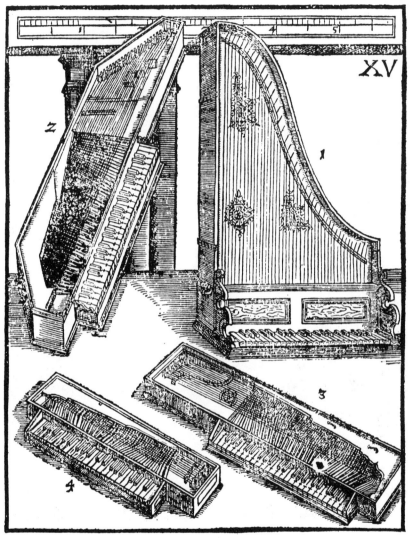

1. Clavicither   2. Clavichord in the Italian measure   3. Common Clavichord
4. Octave Clauichord.

1. Paduan Theorbo   2. Lute with pegs   3. Choir-Lute   4. Quintern   5. Mandürchen
6. Six-stringed Choir-Cither   7. Small English Cither   8. Small Fiddle, called
a Posche.

1. Bandur. 2. Orpheoreon. 3. Penorcon. 4. Italian Lyra da Gamba.

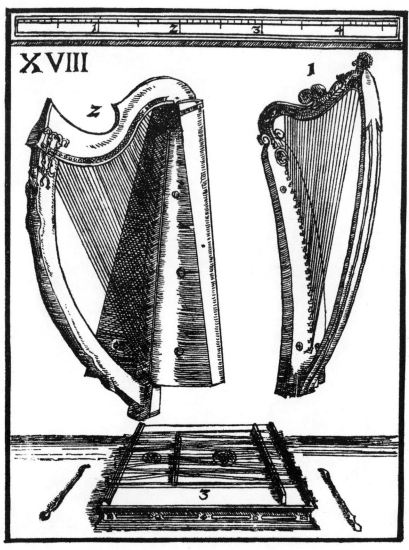

1. Common Harp.   2. Irish Harp with brass strings.   3. Hackbrett or Dulcimer.

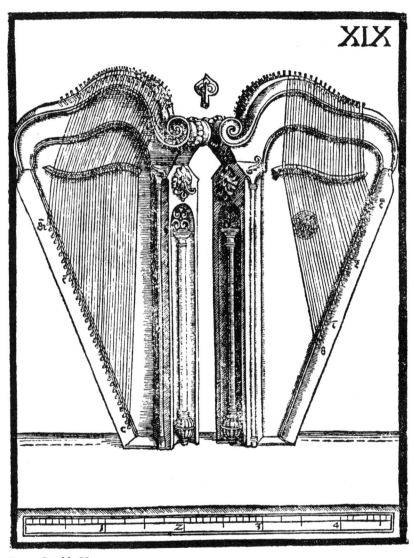

Large Double-Harp.

1./2./3. Viols da Gamba   4. Viola Bastarda   5. Italian Lyra da Braccio.

XXI

1./2. Little Posche [Pochette] Fiddles an octave higher.   3. Discant Violin a fourth higher.   4. Standard Discant Violin.   5. Tenor Violin.   6. Bass Violin.   7. Tromba marina.   8. Scheitholt.

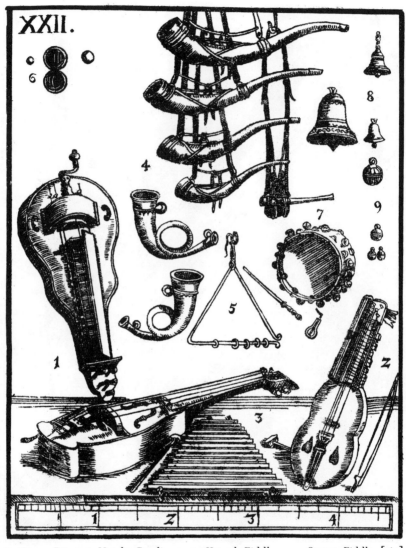

1. Some Peasant Hurdy-Gurdies.   2. Keyed Fiddle.   3. Straw Fiddle [sic]
(xylophone).   4. Hunting Horns.   5. Triangle.   6. Crotales.   7. Little Moorish Tambourine.   8. Bells.   9. Sleighbells.

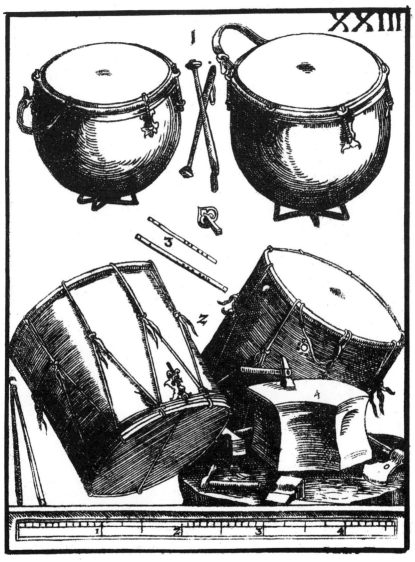

1. Army Drums.   2. Military Drums.   3. Small Swiss Pipes.   4. Anvil.

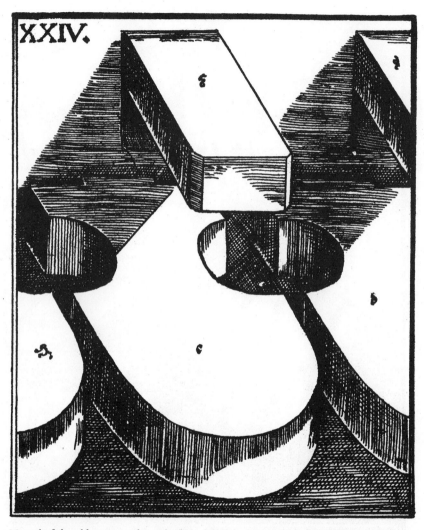

Manual of the old organ in the cathedral of Halberstadt.

The first and second Discant Manuals.

The third Manual.

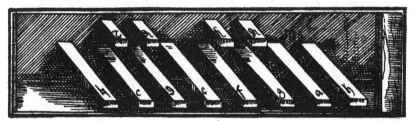

The Pedals.

These are the manuals and pedals of the very large organ in the Halberstadt Cathedral, as they are arranged above each other.

Bellows and Pumpers, as used with the organ at the time.

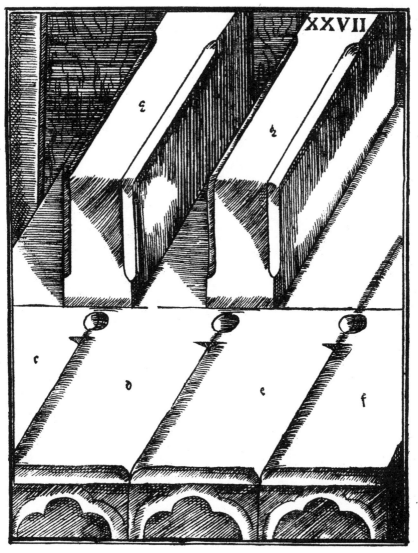

Manual of the old organ at St. Egidio in Braunschweig.

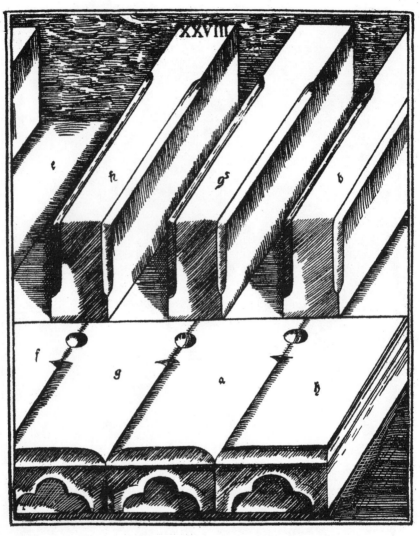

Manual of the Rückpositif in the cited organ of St. Egidio in Braunschweig.

1./2. Satyr Pipes.   3. American Horn or Trumpet.   4. A Ring which the Americans strike much like a Triangle.   5. American Shawm.   6. Cymbals which the Americans play upon like our Bells.   7. A Tambourine which they throw into the air and then catch.   8./9. American Drums.

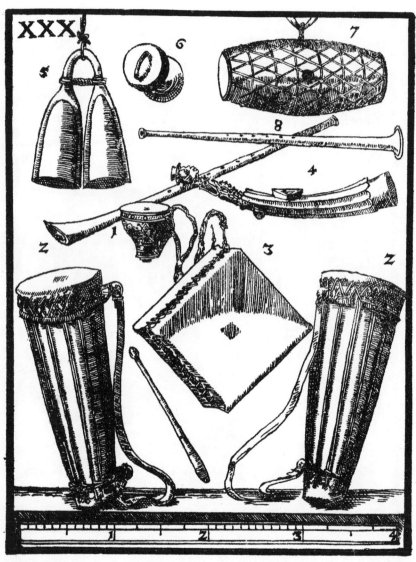

1. A Little Turkish Drum or Kettledrum.   2./3. Muscovite Drums.   4. Indian Ivory Horn.   5. Made from iron, this is played as we play Kettledrums.   6./7./8. Indian Drums and Wind Instruments.

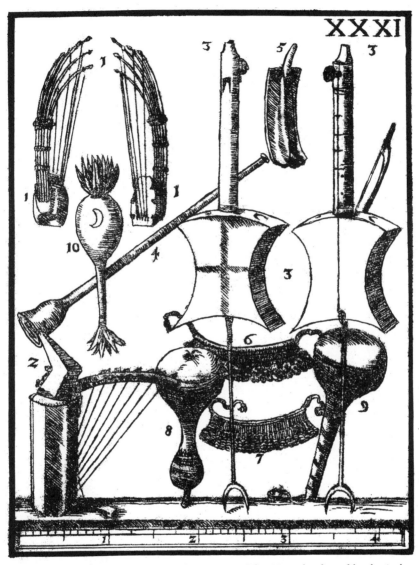

1./2. Indian Instruments sounding like the Harp.   3. This Monochord, used by the Arabs, is a Pipe equipped with a string bowed with a Violin bow.   4. American Trumpet.   5. A Fishbone spanned with two strings on the same pitch.   6./7. Legbands are used by Americans in place of Jingles. They are composed of fruit.   8./9./10. Indian Rattles made from gourds.

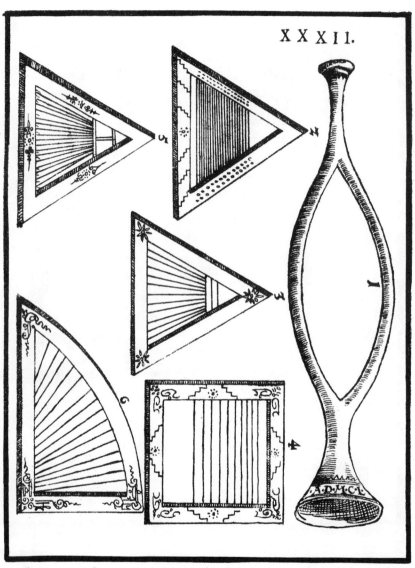

XXXII

1. Chorus.   2. Psaltery.   3./4. Ten-stringed Psalteries.   5./6. Kithara of Hieronymus.

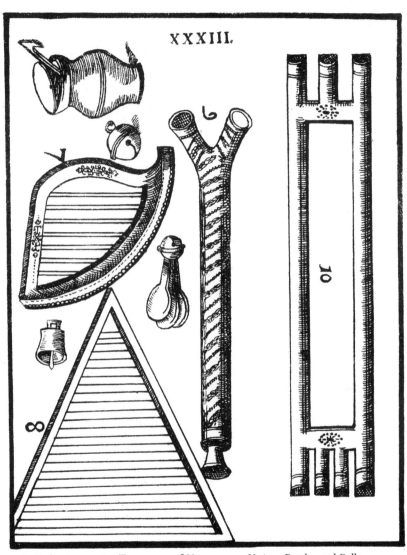

XXXIII.

7./8. Psalteries.   9./10. Tympanum of Hieronymus. Various Rattles and Bells.

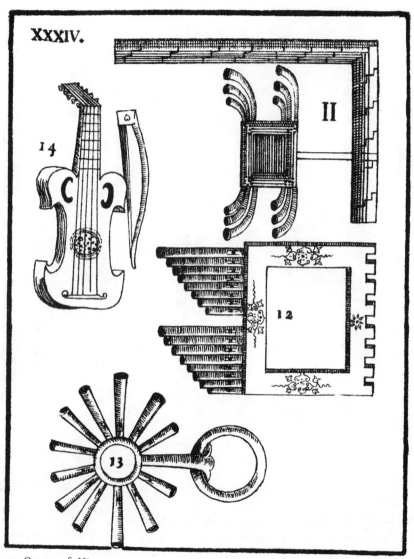

11. Organ of Hieronymus.   12. Fistula of Hieronymus.   13. Cymbalum of
Hieronymus.   14. Old Fiddle.

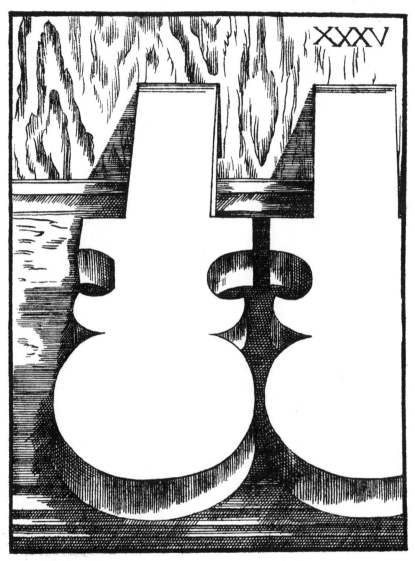

XXXV

Large Magdeburg Key.

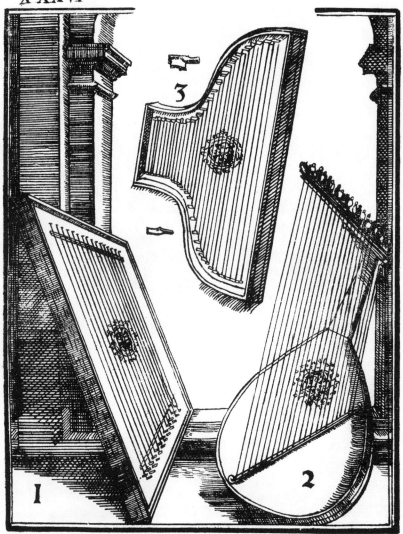

1. A kind of Hackbrett played with the fingers.   2. A unique Lute played in the manner of a Harp.   3. A very old Italian instrument.

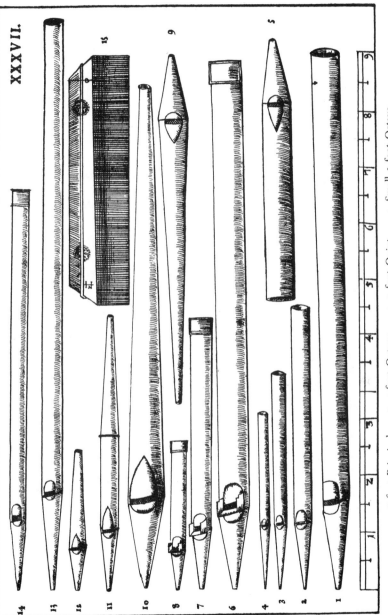

XXXVII.

1. 8-foot Principal.   2. 4-foot Octave.   3. 3-foot Quint.   4. Small 2-foot Octave.
5. 4-foot open Nachthorn. 6. 16-foot Quintadena. 7. 8-foot Quintadena. 8. 4-foot
Nachthorn.   9. Covered 8-foot Lieblich. 10. 8-foot Gemshorn. 11. 4-foot
Spillflute.   12. 2-foot Blockflute.   13. 4-foot Open Flute.   14. 4-foot Covered Flute.

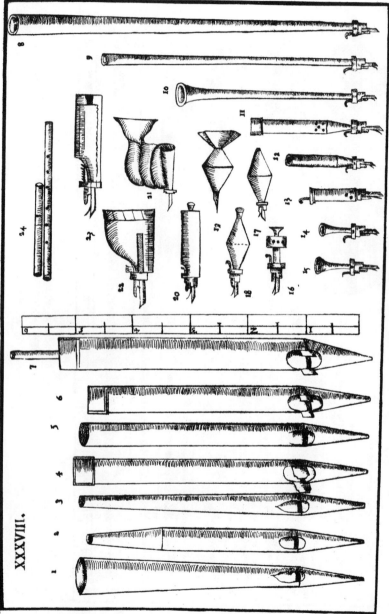

XXXVIII.

1. 4-foot Dulcian. 2. 4-foot Coupleflute. 3. 4-foot Flachflöte 4. 8-foot Small Bardhen. 5. 4-foot Open Flute. 6. 8-foot, Covered. 7. 8-foot Rohrflöte or Hollow Flute. 8. Trumpet. 9. 8-foot Krummhorn. 10. 8-foot Shawm. 11. 16-foot Sordune. 12. Discant Cornet. 13. Rackett, 8 and 16-foot. 14 Brass Regal, 8-foot. 15. Muted Regal. 16./17./18./Krummhorn. 19-23. Peasant Pipes of various kinds. 24 Flute.

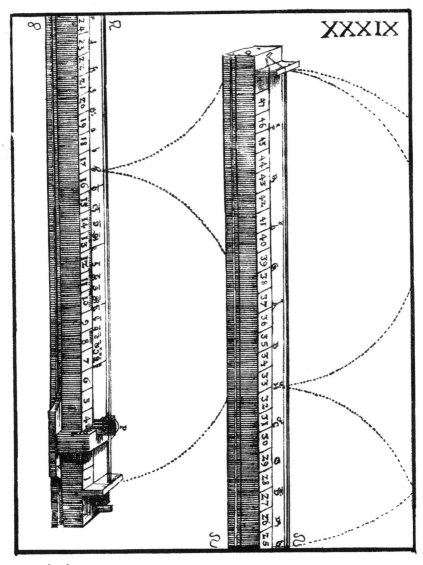

Monochord.

XL.

Cymbals. Number 1: These were fashioned by the ancients from brass into a leaf-like form, termed Umbilicus Veneris in Latin. They had external grips, by means of which they were held. Grasped in each hand, they were struck together and produced a unique ringing sound, which the Romans called tinnitum. Number 3 on plate XLI is also included here.

The other type of Cymbals used by the ancients is shown here under Number 2.

Number 5 is a kind of Drum which may be seen on ancient coins. On top it is even and straight; below it is round (almost like our present kettledrums) and is spanned by an animal hide which was struck by a drumstick and also sometimes by the hand. Numbers 4, 6 and 7 on plate XLI are also included here.

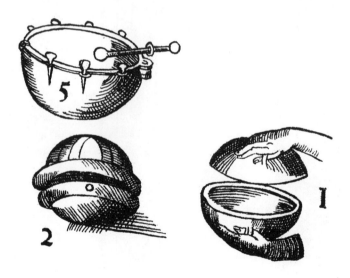

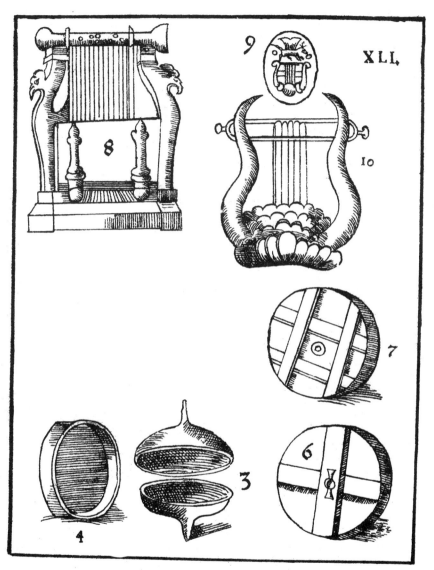

4./6./7. are kinds of Drums, to judge from their external appearance. Number 4 is in the shape of a sieve, and was thus termed a Timpanum Cribri by poets. All are spanned on top with donkey skin or the hides of similar animals.

8./9./10. Unknown and unusual kinds of Lyres, whose characteristics can be seen from above, below, and the side. No 9 is a sketch of a Lyre from an ancient coin; it is comparable to No. 10.

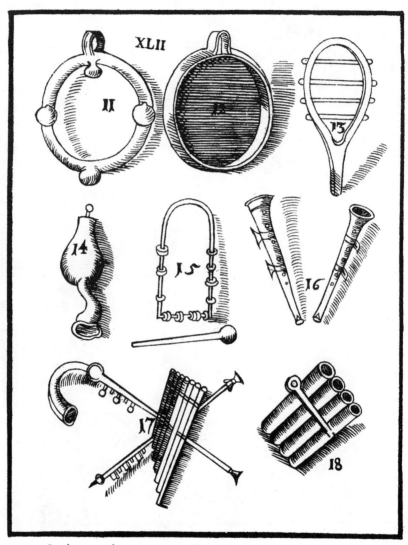

11./12. Sambuca with strings.　13. Sistrum.　14. Utriculus.　15. Crotale or Triangle.　16. Tibias or Fistulas.　17. This is the Fistula or shepherd's pipe, described in Virgil's Bucolica as a fistula with seven conjoined pipes.　18. Cicuta.